Love Through the Ages: The Impact of Famous Love Stories on Modern Relationships

Rajesh Giri

Published by Rajesh Giri, 2023.

While every precaution has been taken in the preparation of this book, the publisher assumes no responsibility for errors or omissions, or for damages resulting from the use of the information contained herein.

LOVE THROUGH THE AGES: THE IMPACT OF FAMOUS LOVE STORIES ON MODERN RELATIONSHIPS

First edition. May 25, 2023.

ISBN: 979-8215222546

Written by Rajesh Giri.

Table of Contents

....1

Introduction 6
Open Talk with Rajesh Kumar Giri 8
Chapter 1: Love in Ancient Times 10
Chapter 2: Romeo and Juliet 16
Chapter 3: Pride and Prejudice.....................................20
Chapter 4: Wuthering Heights......................................26
Chapter 5: Jane Eyre...32
Chapter 6: Anna Karenina 36
Chapter 7: The Great Gatsby 43
Chapter 8: Gone with the Wind....................................48
Chapter 9: Doctor Zhivago..53
Chapter 10: The Notebook 57
Chapter 11: Bridget Jones's Diary.................................63
Chapter 12: Twilight 68
Chapter 13: Fifty Shades of Grey..................................72
Chapter 14: Me Before You...76
Chapter 15: Love through the Ages 81

Dedication

To all the seekers of love, the dreamers of romance, and the believers in the power of human connection,

This book is dedicated to you. Your unwavering commitment to understanding, embracing, and nurturing love has inspired me to embark on this literary journey. Through the pages of "**Love Through the Ages: The Impact of Famous Love Stories on Modern Relationships**," I hope to honor your pursuit of meaningful connections and provide insights that will enrich your lives.

To the lovers who have experienced the soaring heights and the deepest depths of emotion, this book is a tribute to your resilience and courage. May it serve as a reminder that love is an ever-evolving journey, and every experience, whether blissful or challenging, shapes us into stronger, wiser individuals.

To the writers and storytellers who have gifted us with tales of love, both fictional and real, I extend my deepest gratitude. Your words have ignited our imaginations, stirred our hearts, and contributed to the collective understanding of love's complexities. This book stands as a testament to your enduring legacy.

To the scholars, researchers, and psychologists who have delved into the depths of love, decoding its mysteries and shedding light on its impact on our well-being, this book is a humble effort to build upon your invaluable work. It is my hope that the insights shared within these pages contribute to the continued exploration and understanding of love's profound influence.

To my loved ones, who have supported and encouraged me throughout this endeavor, I offer my heartfelt appreciation. Your unwavering belief in my passion for love and literature has been a constant source of inspiration. This book is as much a reflection of your love and support as it is of my own journey.

And finally, to the readers who have entrusted me with their precious time and attention, I am deeply grateful. It is an honor to have the opportunity to share this exploration of love with you. May this book serve as a guiding light, igniting your curiosity, expanding your knowledge, and deepening your connection to the boundless realm of love.

With sincere appreciation and dedication,

Rajesh Giri

The Practical Success Coach

Legal Disclaimer

Copyright@Rajesh Giri - 2023

The information provided in this book is for general informational purposes only. The author and publisher of this book are not responsible for any errors or omissions, or for any consequences resulting from the use of the information contained herein.

The opinions expressed in this book are those of the author and do not necessarily reflect the views of the publisher or any organizations mentioned. The author and publisher are not liable for any damages or losses resulting from the use of this book or the information provided herein.

This book is not intended to provide medical, legal, or professional advice. Readers should consult with their own professionals for any advice related to their specific circumstances.

The names of individuals and places mentioned in this book have been changed to protect their privacy. Any resemblance to real persons or places is purely coincidental.

Preface

Welcome,

Hey there, fellow love enthusiasts!

Welcome to "**Love Through the Ages: The Impact of Famous Love Stories on Modern Relationships.**" Get ready to embark on an extraordinary journey through time as we explore the fascinating world of love and its profound influence on our lives.

This book is all about celebrating the power of love and how it has shaped our understanding of relationships today. Love stories have always held a special place in our hearts, captivating our imaginations and stirring our emotions. They have the incredible ability to transcend time, culture, and language, leaving an indelible mark on the way we perceive and experience love.

In the words of Maya Angelou, "Love recognizes no barriers. It jumps hurdles, leaps fences, penetrates walls to arrive at its destination full of hope." These stories have done just that—breaking down barriers, leaping over obstacles, and inspiring us to believe in the transformative power of love.

So, what can you expect from this love-filled adventure?

Let's dive in and explore the features that make this book a must-read:

• **A journey through time:** We'll travel back through the ages, from ancient civilizations to modern times, discovering how love has evolved and remained a constant force throughout history.

• **Iconic love stories:** We'll unravel the enchanting tales of Romeo and Juliet, Pride and Prejudice, Wuthering Heights, and many more. These stories have touched millions of hearts, and we'll delve deep into their themes, characters, and enduring impact.

• **Thoughtful analysis:** We won't just retell these love stories; we'll dissect them, examining the complexities, motivations, and consequences of love. Through analysis, we'll gain insights into the human psyche and the intricacies of modern relationships.

- **Universal truths:** Love has always been a universal language. We'll explore the timeless truths that resonate across cultures and generations, reminding us that love knows no boundaries.

- **Personal reflections:** As we explore each love story, we'll encourage you to reflect on your own experiences, feelings, and beliefs about love. It's an opportunity to connect with these stories on a personal level and discover how they've impacted your own journey.

- **A guide to navigating modern relationships:** By studying the lessons embedded within these stories, we'll equip you with valuable wisdom to navigate the complexities of modern relationships. Love isn't always a fairy tale, but these stories can offer valuable insights and guidance.

In the words of Nicholas Sparks, "The emotion that can break your heart is sometimes the very one that heals it." Through the ups and downs, the heartaches and triumphs, these love stories have the power to touch us deeply and help us grow as individuals.

So, grab a cozy spot, prepare to be captivated, and let " **Love Through the Ages: The Impact of Famous Love Stories on Modern Relationships** " take you on an unforgettable journey. Remember, as Aristotle wisely said, "Love is composed of a single soul inhabiting two bodies." Together, let's explore the impact of famous love stories on our modern relationships and discover the magic that lies within.

With love,

Rajesh Giri

The Practical Success Coach

Introduction

Love has been a captivating and transformative force throughout human history. From the earliest tales of epic romances to the modern stories that resonate with contemporary audiences, the concept of love has evolved, shaped by cultural, social, and historical contexts. In **"Love Through the Ages: The Impact of Famous Love Stories on Modern Relationships,"** we embark on a journey through time, exploring how famous love stories have influenced and shaped our understanding of love and relationships in the present day.

In this book, we delve into the profound impact that timeless love stories have had on our perceptions, expectations, and experiences of love. We examine the narratives that have captured hearts and minds across centuries and continents, analyzing their themes, characters, and enduring relevance. By examining the archetypal figures, societal norms, and emotional landscapes depicted in these love stories, we gain insight into the complexities of modern relationships.

Each chapter focuses on a different iconic love story and its significance in the broader context of love through the ages. From ancient tales of forbidden love to contemporary explorations of desire, we uncover the universal truths and lessons embedded within these narratives. Through careful analysis and thoughtful reflection, we aim to understand how these stories have shaped our collective consciousness and influenced our own romantic pursuits.

Whether it's Shakespeare's star-crossed lovers in "Romeo and Juliet," the enduring charm of Jane Austen's "Pride and Prejudice," or the tumultuous passions of Emily Brontë's "Wuthering Heights," we explore the motivations, conflicts, and resolutions that have made these stories stand the test of time. We also examine more recent additions to the canon, such as the transformative power of love in Nicholas Sparks' "The Notebook" or the exploration of unconventional desires in E. L. James' "Fifty Shades of Grey."

By studying these influential love stories, we gain a deeper understanding of the complexities and nuances of modern relationships. We explore how these tales have challenged societal norms, inspired personal growth, and shaped our expectations of love. Ultimately, " **Love Through the Ages: The Impact of Famous Love Stories on Modern Relationships** " invites readers to reflect on their own experiences of love and relationships, drawing wisdom from the past to navigate the complexities of the present.

Open Talk with Rajesh Kumar Giri

Hey there, fellow love enthusiasts!

I am absolutely thrilled to present to you "**Love Through the Ages: The Impact of Famous Love Stories on Modern Relationships.**" This book has been a labor of love (pun intended!) and a true passion project for me. I believe it has the potential to be a milestone in enhancing your love life and expanding your knowledge in ways you can't even imagine.

Love is a universal language that has the power to touch our souls and transform our lives. But let's face it, navigating the realm of love and relationships can be challenging. We often find ourselves grappling with questions, doubts, and the complexities of modern romance.

That's where this book comes in to provide you with a roadmap, using the timeless wisdom embedded within famous love stories.

Through the exploration of iconic love stories, we unravel the secrets of love—its joys, its sorrows, its triumphs, and its pitfalls. By analyzing the motivations, conflicts, and resolutions within these narratives, we gain a deeper understanding of ourselves and our own love lives. This book offers a unique blend of literary analysis, psychological insights, and personal reflections to illuminate the path to enhancing your own love life.

But what makes this book truly special is its ability to connect the dots between the past and the present. By studying the impact of these love stories throughout history, we uncover universal truths that transcend time and culture. The knowledge you'll gain from these pages will not only empower you in your relationships but also provide a richer understanding of love's profound influence on our society and the human experience.

I firmly believe that " **Love Through the Ages: The Impact of Famous Love Stories on Modern Relationships** " has the potential to be a milestone in your journey towards a more fulfilling love life. It offers a unique blend of entertainment, introspection, and practical guidance that can be applied in your own relationships. Whether you're single, in a long-term partnership, or just curious about the complexities of love, this book is a treasure trove of insights waiting to be discovered.

So, my dear readers, open your heart, grab a cozy spot, and immerse yourself in the captivating world of " **Love Through the Ages: The Impact of Famous Love Stories on Modern Relationships**." Let it be your companion on a journey of self-discovery, knowledge, and enhanced love life. Embrace the wisdom of the past, and let it guide you towards a brighter, more fulfilling future in matters of the heart.

With love and excitement,

Rajesh Giri

The Practical Success Coach

Chapter 1: Love in Ancient Times

Uncovering the Foundations

Love has been a powerful and enduring force throughout human history, transcending time and cultures.

Love's whispers echo through the ages past,
In ancient realms where histories are vast.
From Mesopotamia, love did arise,
Enchanting hearts beneath Mesopotamian skies.
Egyptian sands, where love held sacred ground,
In afterlife and mortal realms, love found.
Through hieroglyphs, their tales of love unfold,
A bridge between the living and the old.
In Greece, Eros danced in passion's sway,
In search of beauty, love's eternal play.
Plato's wisdom shared the many hues,
From fiery passion to love's intellectual fuse.
Gilgamesh's epic tale, a friendship's reign,
In bonds of love, the hero finds his bane.
Egyptian love poetry, words caress,
Desires aflame, hearts yearning, love's finesse.
In myths and legends, Greece's love did bloom,
Zeus and Hera, Orpheus' mournful tomb.
Romantic customs graced Mesopotamian nights,
Where marriage's dance fused love and family's rights.
Egyptian unions, blending love and fate,
In social ties, love's essence couldn't abate.
Greek love's facets, eros, philia, agape,
A tapestry of bonds, love's vibrant shape.

Ishtar and Tammuz, love's eternal score,
Life's cycle mirrored, love's lore to adore.
Cleopatra and Mark Antony's embrace,
A love affair that time cannot erase.
Eros and Psyche, love's trials unfurled,
Lessons of trust, love's transformative world.
In art and architecture, love displayed,
Mesopotamia, Egypt, Greece portrayed.
Sculptures in stone, reliefs and paintings grand,
Love's beauty captured, brushstroke by hand.
Ancient love's influence, our hearts still feel,
In modern times, its power revealed.
For love transcends the boundaries of time,
A force that shapes our lives, sublime.
Ancient civilizations teach us true,
Love's essence, timeless, forever anew.
In understanding love's ancient embrace,
We find connection, a universal space.
Through cultures and stories, art's vibrant hue,
Love's legacy endures, both ancient and true.
So let us cherish love's enduring flame,
And honor those whose hearts still bear love's name.
For in love's realm, we find our souls aligned,
A testament to love's power, forever enshrined.

Love in Ancient Civilizations

Love in Ancient Mesopotamia

One of the oldest recorded civilizations, Mesopotamia, showcased a multifaceted understanding of love. The Sumerians, who inhabited this ancient land, believed that love was an integral part of their daily lives. Love was not only romantic but also intertwined with religious beliefs. The goddess of love, Inanna, played a significant role in their mythology and cultural practices.

Love in Ancient Egypt

In ancient Egypt, love held a central place in society. Egyptians believed in the power of love to shape both the mortal and the divine realms. Love was often associated with their belief in the afterlife, and it played a crucial role in their funerary practices. The concept of love was deeply connected to their spirituality and their perception of life beyond death.

Love in Ancient Greece

Ancient Greece is renowned for its profound contributions to philosophy, art, and culture. Love, known as "eros," held a special place in Greek society. The Greeks celebrated the passionate and sensual aspects of love, as well as its spiritual and intellectual dimensions. The philosopher Plato explored the various forms of love, emphasizing the pursuit of beauty and wisdom.

Love in Ancient Literature

Love in the Epic of Gilgamesh

The Epic of Gilgamesh, one of the earliest surviving works of literature, provides insights into the ancient Mesopotamian perception of love. This epic poem portrays the profound friendship between Gilgamesh and Enkidu, showcasing the power of love to transform individuals and society.

Love in Egyptian Love Poetry

The ancient Egyptians expressed their emotions and desires through beautiful love poetry. These poems depicted the longing and passion between lovers, offering glimpses into the romantic aspects of ancient Egyptian culture. The words of these love poems continue to captivate readers today.

Love in Greek Mythology

Greek mythology is replete with tales of love, desire, and divine intervention. From the love affair between Zeus and Hera to the tragic story of Orpheus and Eurydice, these myths reflect the complexities of love and its impact on mortal and immortal beings.

Romantic Customs and Practices

Ancient Mesopotamian Marriage and Courtship

Marriage and courtship in ancient Mesopotamia were marked by elaborate rituals and customs. Arranged marriages were common, and weddings were grand affairs. Love and companionship were valued in these unions, but practical considerations and family alliances played significant roles as well.

Egyptian Romantic Traditions

In ancient Egypt, love and marriage were influenced by societal norms and religious beliefs. Pharaohs and nobles often married within their social class to maintain power and prestige. The concept of love extended beyond the romantic, encompassing familial and communal bonds.

Greek Concepts of Love

The Greeks recognized various forms of love, including eros (passionate love), philia (friendship), and agape (unconditional love). Love in ancient Greece encompassed both physical desire and intellectual connection, and it was seen as a transformative force that could elevate individuals and society.

Famous Love Stories from Ancient Times

The Story of Ishtar and Tammuz

Ishtar, the Mesopotamian goddess of love and fertility, had a passionate and tragic love affair with Tammuz. This myth symbolizes the eternal cycle of life, death, and rebirth and serves as a reminder of the power and complexities of love.

The Tale of Cleopatra and Mark Antony

The love story of Cleopatra, the queen of Egypt, and Mark Antony, a Roman general, is an enduring tale of passion and political intrigue. Their union influenced the course of history and captured the imagination of generations.

The Legend of Eros and Psyche

In Greek mythology, the love story of Eros, the god of love, and Psyche, a mortal princess, represents the trials and tribulations that love can endure. It explores themes of trust, perseverance, and the transformative nature of love.

Love in Ancient Art and Architecture

Depictions of Love in Mesopotamian Art

Mesopotamian art provides valuable insights into the ancient civilization's perception of love. Love and romantic themes were depicted in sculptures, reliefs, and jewelry, showcasing the significance of love in their culture.

Love Themes in Egyptian Art

Egyptian art often portrayed scenes of love and intimacy. Paintings on tomb walls and temple reliefs depicted couples embracing, showcasing the importance of love in both mortal and eternal realms.

Greek Sculptures and Paintings of Love

Greek art celebrated love in various forms. Sculptures like the famous statue of Aphrodite, the goddess of love, and paintings like "The Birth of Venus" by Botticelli captured the beauty and allure of love in ancient Greece.

The Influence of Ancient Love on Modern Relationships

The legacy of ancient love continues to resonate in modern relationships. Lessons from ancient civilizations remind us of the enduring nature of love and its impact on our lives. By understanding the foundations of love in ancient times, we gain a deeper appreciation for the complexities and transformative power of love today.

Conclusion

Love has been an intrinsic part of human existence since ancient times. The cultures and civilizations of the past had their unique perspectives on love, which shaped their customs, literature, art, and societal norms. Exploring love in ancient Mesopotamia, Egypt, and Greece, as well as the famous love stories and artistic expressions of the time, provides us with a deeper understanding of the universal and timeless nature of love.

Chapter 2: Romeo and Juliet

A Tale of Passionate Devotion

"Romeo and Juliet" is a timeless tragic love story that has captivated audiences for centuries. Set in the picturesque city of Verona, the play explores the profound and passionate devotion between the two young lovers, Romeo and Juliet.

"Romeo and Juliet" is perhaps William Shakespeare's most famous play, known for its tragic portrayal of two young lovers caught in the midst of a bitter family feud. The story is an embodiment of passionate devotion, as Romeo and Juliet defy societal expectations and risk everything for their love. It is a tale that transcends time and continues to resonate with audiences of all generations.

In Verona's fair city, a tale unfurled,
Of two young lovers, their hearts swiftly twirled.
Romeo and Juliet, their names renowned,
Their love's flame, a passion unbound.
Verona's streets, where love's drama took flight,
A feud between families, casting shadows of night.
Montague and Capulet, their hatred ran deep,
Yet love's sweet allure, their hearts couldn't keep.
Love at first sight, their eyes did meet,
In that moonlit moment, destiny sweet.
A balcony scene, vows whispered on high,
Love's declaration beneath a starry sky.
Forbidden love, a dangerous dance,
Fueled by passion's fire, they took a chance.
Society's expectations, they dared to defy,
For love's relentless call, they were willing to die.

Passion's power, a flame uncontrolled,
Guiding their hearts, a story to be told.
Their love, a tempest in a world torn apart,
A testament to the depths of the human heart.
Tragic consequences, a bitter twist of fate,
Misunderstandings and missteps sealed their cruel state.
Through poison's touch, they found their final rest,
A love eternal, forever blessed.
Love, fate, and destiny, themes intertwined,
Light and darkness, symbols deeply enshrined.
From Shakespeare's quill, this tale did unfold,
An enduring masterpiece, a story to be told.
Through centuries past, its impact remains,
In literature, theater, its spirit sustains.
Romeo and Juliet, love's tragic song,
Forever echoing, hearts forever long.
In Verona's fair city, their love still prevails,
A testament to love's triumph and its travails.
May their tale remind us of love's precious grace,
And the enduring power of love's embrace.

The Setting of Verona

THE PLAY IS SET IN the city of Verona, Italy, a place renowned for its romantic allure. Verona serves as the backdrop for the unfolding drama, enhancing the atmosphere of forbidden love and destiny. In addition to its romantic charm, Verona holds historical significance, as it was a city marked by intense political and social rivalries during Shakespeare's time.

The Characters

At the heart of "Romeo and Juliet" are the two star-crossed lovers, Romeo and Juliet. Romeo, a young Montague, is characterized by his impulsive nature and unwavering devotion. Juliet, a Capulet, is portrayed as a fiercely independent and intelligent young woman. Their love is intense and all-consuming, leading them to make choices that have fatal consequences.

Love at First Sight

One of the most iconic scenes in the play is the balcony scene, where Romeo and Juliet declare their love for each other. The balcony scene represents the epitome of romanticism, as the lovers exchange heartfelt vows and promises. Their immediate and deep connection illustrates the power of love at first sight, defying rationality and societal conventions.

Forbidden Love

The love between Romeo and Juliet is further complicated by the long-standing feud between their families, the Montagues and the Capulets. This animosity creates a forbidden love that intensifies the passion between the two lovers. Despite the risks and the potential consequences, Romeo and Juliet are willing to defy societal expectations and pursue their love at any cost.

The Power of Passion

Passionate love is a central theme in "Romeo and Juliet." The play explores the transformative and all-consuming nature of love, depicting it as a force that compels the characters to act in unpredictable ways. The passion between Romeo and Juliet drives them to make impulsive decisions, leading to a chain of events that ultimately seals their tragic fate.

Tragic Consequences

As with many of Shakespeare's tragedies, "Romeo and Juliet" culminates in the devastating deaths of the two young lovers. Their untimely demise is a result of a series of unfortunate events, misunderstandings, and fatal mistakes. The play serves as a reminder of the consequences of unchecked passion and the destructive power of societal divisions.

Themes and Symbols

"Romeo and Juliet" explores several themes, including love, fate, and destiny. The theme of love, in its various forms and complexities, is pervasive throughout the play. Fate and destiny are also recurring motifs, highlighting the idea that the lovers were destined to meet and face their tragic end. Additionally, symbols such as light and darkness, poison, and the stars are woven into the narrative, adding depth and richness to the story.

Impact and Influence

"Romeo and Juliet" has had a lasting impact on literature, theater, and popular culture. Countless adaptations and interpretations of the play have been created, both on stage and in film. The story's themes of love, passion, and sacrifice continue to resonate with audiences worldwide, making it an enduring classic.

Conclusion

"Romeo and Juliet" remains a testament to the power of love and the consequences of unyielding devotion. The play's exploration of passionate love, forbidden romance, and tragic circumstances continues to captivate audiences, highlighting the universal nature of human emotions. Through its timeless themes and memorable characters, "Romeo and Juliet" remains a masterpiece of literature.

Chapter 3: Pride and Prejudice

Breaking Societal Norms for Love

Love is a powerful emotion that knows no boundaries. However, society often imposes its expectations and norms on individuals, dictating whom they should love and how relationships should unfold. In Jane Austen's classic novel, Pride and Prejudice, the characters defy societal conventions, challenging the limitations placed on love.

Love's melody, an everlasting tune,
Defying societal chains, its power strewn.
In Austen's Pride and Prejudice we find,
Characters who challenge love's confined.
Society's Influence on Love's Path
Expectations and norms, a society's wrath,
Dictating whom to love, how hearts shall roam.
Shaping perceptions, love's essence to disown.
Gender Roles, Love's Tangled Knot
For women demure, men assertive sought.
Traditional roles, barriers they create,
Love's true path obscured by societal dictate.
Class and Status, Society's Divide
Obstacles arise, love's crossing denied.
The pressure to conform, to marry the same,
Class divisions upheld, love's flame tamed.
Pride and Prejudice, Austen's Tale
Unfolds in English fields, where hearts prevail.
The Bennet family, their story takes flight,
Elizabeth and Mr. Darcy, their love's respite.
Elizabeth Bennet, a Rebel Soul

Defying norms, her heart in control.
She seeks love's truth, not wealth's embrace,
Inspiring readers to challenge their place.
Mr. Darcy, Overcoming Prejudice's Veil
A transformation unfolds, his barriers pale.
His pride and judgments, he learns to shed,
Love's genuine essence, he comes to tread.
Boundaries Transcended, Love's Realm Expands
Pride and Prejudice, love's audacious stands.
Forbidden connections, choices complex,
Societal constraints shattered, love's true vortex.
Class Barriers, Love's Journey Brave
Elizabeth and Mr. Darcy, a love they crave.
Defying societal expectations, they soar,
Proving love's strength, its power to explore.
Love's Reach, Beyond Expectations Soar
Other characters defy, love's wings they bore.
Jane and Bingley, Lydia and Wickham's flight,
Love's unconventional triumphs, hearts alight.
Lessons for Modern Souls
In Pride and Prejudice, wisdom unrolls.
Challenge societal norms, be true and free,
Embrace love's authenticity, let hearts be.
Love in the 21st Century's Glow
Society's chains, still love's winds do blow.
Pride and Prejudice, a timeless plea,
For love's liberation, let souls be free.
Embrace Individuality, Love's Purest Core
Stay true to oneself, let hearts explore.
Authentic connections, genuine and deep,
Shattering expectations, love's secrets to reap.
Stereotypes and Expectations, Face Them Bold

In love's pursuit, let judgments withhold.
Beyond class and prejudice, let hearts align,
Pride and Prejudice's legacy, love's design.
In the end, love's power resounds,
Pride and Prejudice's symphony abounds.
Break free from society's confining walls,
Love's boundless song, in hearts it enthralls.

The Influence of Society on Relationships

Societal expectations hold considerable influence over relationships. From an early age, individuals are bombarded with messages about how they should behave, whom they should marry, and what constitutes a successful partnership. These societal norms shape our perceptions of love and influence the choices we make in our romantic lives.

Gender Roles and Expectations

Traditional gender roles play a significant role in dictating societal norms surrounding love. Women are often expected to be demure, obedient, and seek security in marriage, while men are expected to be assertive and provide for their families. These gender expectations can create barriers to finding true love when individuals feel compelled to conform to predetermined roles.

Class and Social Status

Class and social status have long been determinants of acceptable relationships in many societies. The divide between social classes can create significant obstacles for those who dare to love across class boundaries. The pressure to marry within one's social stratum can stifle genuine connections and perpetuate societal divisions.

Pride and Prejudice: A Classic Love Story

Jane Austen's Pride and Prejudice provides a captivating narrative that challenges societal norms and expectations. The novel centers around the spirited Elizabeth Bennet, who defies conventional expectations for women of her time, and Mr. Darcy, a wealthy and initially haughty gentleman who learns to overcome his own prejudices.

Overview of Pride and Prejudice

Set in the English countryside during the early 19th century, Pride and Prejudice tells the story of the Bennet family and their five daughters. The novel explores themes of love, marriage, social class, and societal expectations, with a particular focus on the relationship between Elizabeth Bennet and Mr. Darcy.

Elizabeth Bennet: Challenging the Norms

Elizabeth Bennet stands as a strong-willed and independent woman who defies societal norms of her time. She refuses to succumb to societal pressures to marry solely for financial security, instead valuing love, respect, and intellectual compatibility. Elizabeth's refusal to conform challenges the status quo and inspires readers to question the limitations placed on women in society.

Mr. Darcy: Overcoming Prejudice

Mr. Darcy, initially portrayed as proud and aloof, experiences a transformation throughout the novel. He confronts his own prejudices and learns to appreciate Elizabeth's intelligence, wit, and independent spirit. His journey illustrates the importance of looking beyond superficial judgments and societal expectations in matters of the heart.

Love Transcending Boundaries

Pride and Prejudice showcases love that defies societal boundaries, challenging the notion that love should conform to societal norms. The novel presents various examples of love that surpass societal expectations and defy the constraints imposed by class and prejudice.

Forbidden Love

The theme of forbidden love permeates Pride and Prejudice, adding complexity to the characters' relationships. The societal disapproval of certain romantic connections forces characters to make difficult choices and face the consequences of defying societal norms. This exploration of forbidden love highlights the significance of love that transcends societal limitations.

Breaking through Class Barriers

Class differences serve as a central conflict in Pride and Prejudice, with characters navigating the challenges of love across social strata. Elizabeth's relationship with Mr. Darcy, for instance, requires them to confront societal expectations and overcome the prejudices associated with class differences. Their love story demonstrates that genuine connections can be forged despite societal barriers.

Love Beyond Social Expectations

Pride and Prejudice also features other characters who defy social expectations in their pursuit of love. Jane Bennet's affection for Mr. Bingley and Lydia Bennet's elopement with Mr. Wickham challenge the conventions of their time. These instances of love beyond social expectations underscore the idea that true happiness can be found when individuals prioritize their own feelings over societal judgments.

Lessons for Modern Society

Pride and Prejudice continues to resonate with readers in the 21st century, providing valuable lessons on love, relationships, and societal expectations. The novel encourages individuals to challenge societal norms and embrace love without prejudice.

Love in the 21st Century

In the modern era, societal expectations still shape our perceptions of love. Pride and Prejudice serves as a reminder that true love can transcend societal constraints and flourish when individuals prioritize their own happiness and fulfillment.

Embracing Individuality and Authenticity

Elizabeth Bennet's character inspires individuals to embrace their individuality and be authentic in their relationships. By staying true to oneself and refusing to conform to societal expectations, one can build meaningful and genuine connections based on mutual respect and understanding.

Challenging Stereotypes and Expectations

Pride and Prejudice urges readers to question and challenge stereotypes and expectations imposed by society. It encourages individuals to look beyond superficial judgments, social class, and prejudices in their pursuit of love. By defying societal norms, one can find a love that is authentic and fulfilling.

Conclusion

Pride and Prejudice beautifully depicts the power of love in breaking societal norms. Through the characters of Elizabeth Bennet and Mr. Darcy, the novel showcases the transformative journey of defying expectations and embracing love without prejudice. In a world where societal norms often limit and confine relationships, Pride and Prejudice serves as a timeless reminder that true love knows no boundaries.

Chapter 4: Wuthering Heights

The Dark Side of Love

In the realm of classic literature, few novels can rival the enduring appeal and dark allure of Emily Brontë's masterpiece, "Wuthering Heights." This novel takes readers on a tumultuous journey through the Yorkshire moors, exploring the depths of human passion and the consequences of unrestrained love. With its complex characters, haunting setting, and captivating storyline, "Wuthering Heights" delves into the dark side of love, revealing the destructive power it holds.

Within the realm of prose so grand,
A masterpiece in Brontë's hand.
"Wuthering Heights," its dark allure,
Unrestrained love, its depths secure.
Romantic elements, passion's fire,
Forbidden desires, hearts' desire.
Heathcliff and Catherine, love untamed,
Transcending norms, longing inflamed.
Dark love's side, its shadows cast,
Destructive force that holds love fast.
Obsession's grasp, consuming whole,
Heathcliff's vengeance takes its toll.
Revenge entwined with love's despair,
A cycle spun, hearts left threadbare.
Conflict born from love's embrace,
Jealousy, rivalry, hearts misplaced.
Characters complex, each unique,
Heathcliff brooding, torments seek.
Catherine torn, conflicted soul,

Human nature's depths unroll.
Class divisions, barriers imposed,
Love thwarted, desire enclosed.
Societal norms, love's foe,
Shattering hearts, dreams laid low.
Nature's backdrop, moors untamed,
Mirror turbulent love unchained.
Symbolism woven, wild and stark,
Unsettling love leaves its mark.
Supernatural specters haunting sight,
Eerie visions in the night.
Love's darkness, a chilling breath,
Haunting souls long after death.
Death's role, love's consequence dire,
Self-destruction, relationships expire.
Tragic tale of love's demise,
Characters lost, love's sacrifice.
Unconventional narrative structure weaves,
Nested tales, perspectives cleave.
Complexity mirrored, relationships entwined,
Dark love's labyrinth, secrets confined.
Enduring legacy, timeless appeal,
"Wuthering Heights" hearts still steal.
Passion, obsession, revenge's trace,
A classic that time can't erase.
Literary criticism's vast array,
Interpretations blooming, minds at play.
Deeper meanings found, revelations unfold,
"Wuthering Heights" studied, its story retold.
In conclusion, "Wuthering Heights" stands,
As a testament to love's shifting sands.
Darkness and light entwined in its core,

A masterpiece of love's depths explored.

The Romantic Elements in Wuthering Heights

Before delving into the darker side of love in "Wuthering Heights," it is essential to acknowledge the presence of romantic elements within the narrative. The novel encompasses intense emotions, forbidden desires, and passionate relationships that ignite the plot. Through the characters of Heathcliff and Catherine Earnshaw, Brontë presents a love that transcends societal norms and conventional boundaries, evoking a sense of longing and tragedy.

The Dark Side of Love in Wuthering Heights

While love is often associated with positive emotions, "Wuthering Heights" presents a different perspective, exploring the destructive nature of certain forms of love. Brontë delves into the complexities of human relationships, showcasing the detrimental effects of obsession, possessiveness, and unrequited love. The novel challenges traditional notions of love, offering a stark portrayal of its dark consequences.

The Destructive Nature of Obsessive Love

One of the central themes in "Wuthering Heights" is the destructive power of obsessive love. Heathcliff's infatuation with Catherine drives him to extreme actions, manipulating and seeking revenge on those who stand in the way of their love. This obsession consumes Heathcliff, transforming him into a vengeful and tormented character who stops at nothing to possess what he desires.

The Theme of Revenge

Love and revenge intertwine in "Wuthering Heights," highlighting the destructive cycle fueled by passionate emotions. Characters in the novel often resort to revenge as a response to heartbreak or betrayal. The desire for retribution drives the narrative, further emphasizing the darker side of love and the lasting impact it can have on individuals and their relationships.

Love as a Source of Conflict

Brontë explores the tumultuous nature of love, illustrating how it can be a source of conflict. In "Wuthering Heights," various love triangles and unrequited affections create tension and turmoil among the characters. Love becomes a catalyst for jealousy, rivalry, and manipulation, revealing the complexity and fragility of human relationships.

The Complex Characters in Wuthering Heights

The characters in "Wuthering Heights" are intricately developed, each embodying different aspects of love and its consequences. From the brooding and tormented Heathcliff to the spirited and conflicted Catherine, Brontë crafts characters that reflect the complexities of human nature. These multi-dimensional portrayals contribute to the novel's exploration of the dark side of love.

The Influence of Social Class

Another aspect that adds depth to the portrayal of love in "Wuthering Heights" is the influence of social class. The novel explores the barriers and limitations imposed by societal expectations, showing how love can be thwarted by rigid class divisions. Brontë challenges the notion that love conquers all, emphasizing the detrimental impact of societal norms on personal relationships.

Nature and Setting as Symbolism

The wild and untamed Yorkshire moors serve as a backdrop for the intense emotions and turbulent relationships depicted in the novel. The setting of "Wuthering Heights" reflects the characters' inner turmoil and contributes to the overall atmosphere of the story. Nature, with its unpredictable and harsh elements, becomes a symbol of the characters' turbulent emotions and the destructive power of their love.

The Supernatural Elements

Brontë infuses supernatural elements into the narrative, adding an eerie and mysterious dimension to the novel. The ghostly appearances and visions in "Wuthering Heights" heighten the sense of darkness and foreboding. These supernatural occurrences further emphasize the unsettling nature of love and its ability to haunt individuals long after death.

The Role of Death

Death plays a significant role in "Wuthering Heights," serving as a reminder of the consequences of unrestrained love. Brontë explores the idea that love can lead to self-destruction and the demise of relationships. The specter of death hovers over the characters, ultimately shaping their actions and contributing to the tragic nature of the story.

The Unconventional Structure of the Novel

"Wuthering Heights" stands out not only for its themes but also for its unconventional narrative structure. The novel is presented as a series of nested narratives, with multiple perspectives and timelines interwoven. This fragmented structure mirrors the complexity and intricacy of the characters' relationships, further enhancing the exploration of the dark side of love.

The Enduring Legacy of Wuthering Heights

Since its publication in 1847, "Wuthering Heights" has captivated readers and influenced countless works of literature. The novel's enduring legacy lies in its portrayal of the darker aspects of love and its ability to transcend time and cultural boundaries. Brontë's exploration of passion, obsession, and revenge continues to resonate with readers today, making "Wuthering Heights" a timeless classic.

The Impact on Literary Criticism

" Wuthering Heights" has sparked extensive literary criticism and analysis, further illuminating its exploration of the dark side of love. Scholars and critics have delved into the complexities of the novel, uncovering hidden meanings and interpretations. The critical discourse surrounding "Wuthering Heights" showcases the profound impact it has had on the study of literature and its enduring relevance.

Conclusion

In conclusion, "Wuthering Heights" is a haunting and evocative novel that explores the dark side of love. Through its intense characters, captivating setting, and thought-provoking themes, Emily Brontë crafts a narrative that delves into the destructive power of passion, obsession, and revenge. The novel's enduring legacy lies in its ability to confront readers with the complex and often unsettling aspects of human relationships. "Wuthering Heights" remains a testament to the enduring allure of dark love stories that continue to captivate audiences across generations.

Chapter 5: Jane Eyre

Finding Love in Adversity

Jane Eyre, a timeless literary masterpiece written by Charlotte Brontë, has captivated readers for generations. Its enduring appeal lies not only in its compelling narrative but also in its exploration of love and resilience in the face of adversity.

In Charlotte Brontë's prose divine,
A masterpiece through passing time.
"Jane Eyre," a tale profound,
Love and resilience it does expound.
Adversity marked Jane's early days,
Orphaned, mistreated in cruel ways.
Lowood School brought trials anew,
Yet knowledge and spirit she would pursue.
At Thornfield Hall, her fate did shift,
Encountering Mr. Rochester's cryptic rift.
Their connection grew, defying norms,
Love blossomed amidst life's storms.
Obstacles emerged, challenges untold,
Societal expectations, love's stronghold.
But Jane's growth and self-realization,
Asserting her desires, a revelation.
Their love tested, a revelation stark,
Jane faced choices that left a mark.
Society's chains could not bind,
Love triumphed, freeing heart and mind.
Jane's independence found its flight,
A journey of self, her own light.

Love's transformative power, its allure,
Healing wounds, embracing the pure.
"Jane Eyre" resonates, its message clear,
Love and resilience conquer fear.
Through adversity, Jane's spirit soared,
Inspiring readers to embrace their own accord.
In Brontë's words, a timeless tale,
Love's triumphs, resilience prevail.
"Jane Eyre" reminds us still,
Love's power to heal, transform, fulfill.
In conclusion, "Jane Eyre" remains,
A testament to love's enduring reigns.
Brontë's masterpiece, a beacon bright,
Love, resilience, its guiding light.

Exploring Jane's early life: An orphan in adversity

A difficult childhood

From the very beginning, Jane's life was marked by hardship. Orphaned at a young age, she was subjected to a harsh upbringing at the hands of her aunt and cousins. Her isolation and mistreatment fueled her resilience and shaped her character, setting the stage for her remarkable journey.

Jane's experiences at the Lowood School

Sent away to Lowood School, Jane faced further trials and tribulations. The school's strict regime and harsh conditions seemed unbearable at times. However, it was during her time at Lowood that Jane discovered her thirst for knowledge, developed enduring friendships, and cultivated her indomitable spirit.

The power of resilience and self-discovery

Jane's journey to Thornfield Hall

After leaving Lowood, Jane secured a position as a governess at Thornfield Hall. Here, in the heart of the Yorkshire moors, her life took an unexpected turn. Jane's encounter with the enigmatic and brooding

Mr. Rochester would forever change her path, igniting a deep and profound connection.

The enigmatic Mr. Rochester

Mr. Rochester, with his complex and mysterious demeanor, captivated Jane from the moment they met. Their shared intellectual pursuits and the genuine connection they formed transcended societal conventions. However, beneath the surface, secrets and obstacles lurked, challenging their budding relationship.

Jane's growth and self-realization

Throughout her time at Thornfield Hall, Jane experienced tremendous personal growth. She confronted her own insecurities, challenged societal expectations, and discovered her worth as an individual. In the process, she became more confident, assertive, and self-assured, unafraid to assert her own desires and needs.

Love amidst challenges

The blossoming relationship between Jane and Mr. Rochester

Jane and Mr. Rochester's relationship evolved slowly but passionately. Their intellectual connection deepened into a profound love that defied societal norms. Their shared moments of vulnerability and understanding created a bond that seemed unbreakable.

The obstacles they face

However, their love was not without its challenges. A revelation threatened to shatter their happiness, forcing Jane to make a heart-wrenching decision. The choices they faced tested the strength of their love and forced them to confront their own moral dilemmas.

The impact of societal expectations

The rigid social hierarchy and societal expectations of the Victorian era loomed large over Jane and Mr. Rochester's relationship. Their differing social statuses and the disapproval of others added further complexity and obstacles to their path. Yet, their love persevered, defying the constraints imposed by society.

The transformative power of love

The revelation at Thornfield Hall

In the face of adversity and personal sacrifice, Jane's unwavering love and sense of duty prevailed. A shocking revelation changed the course of events, challenging Jane to reevaluate her priorities and make difficult choices. This pivotal moment set the stage for her transformation and ultimate liberation.

Jane's newfound independence

With the weight of her past lifted, Jane found the strength to embrace her newfound independence. She embarked on a journey of self-discovery, forging her own path and pursuing her passions. Jane's ability to find love in adversity not only transformed her own life but also inspired readers to embrace their own resilience and inner strength.

Love's ability to heal and transform

"Jane Eyre" reminds us of love's transformative power. Through the trials and tribulations faced by Jane and Mr. Rochester, we witness the profound healing and personal growth that love can bring. Their love story serves as a testament to the resilience of the human spirit and the capacity for love to transcend all obstacles.

Conclusion

In "Jane Eyre," Charlotte Brontë weaves a tale of love, resilience, and self-discovery that continues to resonate with readers today. Jane's journey from adversity to love and independence showcases the triumph of the human spirit over challenging circumstances. It reminds us that even in the darkest of times, love has the power to heal, transform, and inspire.

Chapter 6: Anna Karenina

Love and Consequences

Leo Tolstoy's masterpiece, "Anna Karenina," delves into the complex realms of love, passion, and the repercussions of one's choices. Set against the backdrop of 19th-century Russia, this timeless novel explores the intricacies of human emotions and the consequences that unfold when societal norms collide with personal desires. Through the captivating story of Anna Karenina, Tolstoy presents a compelling narrative that continues to resonate with readers today.

In Tolstoy's realm, a tale unfolds,
"Anna Karenina," its story holds.
Love, passion, choices intertwine,
A timeless novel, emotions entwine.
Anna's life, a loveless plight,
Trapped in a marriage, devoid of light.
Vronsky's charm awakens desire's flame,
A passionate affair, a life untamed.
Anna, a complex soul, torn inside,
Yearning for love, societal norms collide.
19th-century Russia's societal sway,
Confronting desires, the price to pay.
Love and marriage, a delicate dance,
Tolstoy's lens, a nuanced glance.
Anna and Vronsky, forbidden love's course,
Defying conventions, a passionate force.
Consequences ripple, beyond their sight,
Love's impact spreads, with every plight.
Societal expectations, pressures immense,

Straining relationships, tearing down defense.
Hypocrisy and judgment, society's plight,
As Anna and Vronsky face scrutiny's might.
Emotional turmoil, guilt seeping through,
Consequences unfold, their love they rue.
Anna's choices, a moral strife,
Duty and desire, battling for life.
Leaving behind, husband and son,
Pursuing love's fire, a life undone.
Choices reverberate, their aftermath profound,
Love's complexities, Tolstoy expounds.
Tragic endings mark this tale of woe,
While hope arises, in Levin and Kitty's glow.
"Anna Karenina" offers reflections deep,
On love's nature, the choices we keep.
A mirror to our souls, it invites introspection,
Confronting our understanding, igniting reflection.
In conclusion, Tolstoy's masterpiece sublime,
"Anna Karenina," a narrative prime.
Love's consequences, its complexities explored,
A timeless tale, our hearts it's scored.

The Story of Anna Karenina

A Brief Overview

"Anna Karenina" follows the life of the eponymous character, a married woman trapped in a loveless and unfulfilling marriage with her husband, Alexei Karenin. As the story progresses, Anna's path intersects with Count Vronsky, a charming and dashing officer who awakens her dormant desires. Igniting a passionate affair, Anna embarks on a journey filled with love, betrayal, and the weighty consequences that come with her choices.

Anna Karenina's Characterization

Tolstoy masterfully crafts Anna's character as a multifaceted individual torn between societal expectations and her own yearnings for love and freedom. She represents the turmoil many individuals face when trapped in unhappy relationships and the lengths they go to pursue genuine happiness. Anna's complexities make her a relatable and compelling protagonist, inviting readers to empathize with her struggles and question the rigid norms of society.

The Setting and Time Period

"Anna Karenina" is set in 19th-century Russia, a time when societal conventions heavily dictated one's actions and choices. Tolstoy skillfully uses this backdrop to explore the clash between personal desires and the expectations imposed by a conservative society. The aristocratic society depicted in the novel serves as a microcosm, showcasing the complexities of love and the consequences that arise when individuals challenge societal norms.

Love in Anna Karenina

Love and Marriage

Tolstoy examines the institution of marriage and the often complex relationship between love and matrimony. In the novel, love is portrayed as a powerful force that can both liberate and destroy individuals. The stark contrast between Anna's loveless marriage and her passionate affair with Vronsky highlights the consequences of pursuing one's desires outside the confines of societal expectations.

Anna and Vronsky's Forbidden Love

Anna and Vronsky's relationship serves as the central focus of the novel, epitomizing the forbidden love that blooms amidst societal restrictions. Their intense connection challenges the boundaries set by their respective commitments and exposes the consequences of defying societal norms. Tolstoy delves into the emotional complexities of their affair, illustrating the turmoil and sacrifices experienced by both parties.

The Consequences of Love

Tolstoy delves deep into the consequences of love, revealing the ripple effects it has on not only the individuals involved but also those around them. As Anna and Vronsky's relationship becomes increasingly public, they face judgment, isolation, and internal turmoil. The consequences of their actions extend beyond their personal lives, affecting their families, friends, and even the broader society in which they reside.

Society's Impact on Love

Social Expectations

Tolstoy explores the influence of societal expectations on individuals' choices and actions. In "Anna Karenina," societal norms act as a stifling force, dictating the roles and obligations of individuals within relationships. The pressure to conform to societal expectations drives many characters to suppress their desires, leading to a clash between personal happiness and societal obligations.

Obligations and Responsibilities

The novel highlights the burdensome responsibilities individuals face within their societal roles. Anna's position as a wife and mother contrasts with her desires for personal fulfillment, exposing the tension between duty and personal happiness. Tolstoy prompts readers to question whether it is possible to navigate these conflicting responsibilities without sacrificing one's own well-being.

Hypocrisy and Judgment

Tolstoy vividly depicts the hypocrisy and judgment prevalent within society. Anna and Vronsky face scrutiny and condemnation from the high society they once belonged to, while those who cast judgment themselves harbor their own secrets and transgressions. This examination of societal double standards challenges readers to reflect on their own biases and the impact of judgment on individuals pursuing love.

Emotional Turmoil and Consequences

Betrayal and Guilt

Tolstoy delves into the emotional turmoil experienced by Anna as her affair with Vronsky unfolds. The weight of her betrayal toward her husband, Karenin, and the guilt that accompanies it plague her conscience. This internal struggle showcases the psychological impact of one's actions and the consequences of betraying trust in pursuit of love.

Anna's Internal Struggles

Anna battles her inner demons throughout the novel, torn between her desires for love and the societal expectations placed upon her. Her internal struggles highlight the psychological toll of living a double life and the psychological complexities of pursuing forbidden love. Tolstoy captures Anna's psychological journey with depth, ensuring readers feel connected to her plight.

Relationships and Family Dynamics

The consequences of Anna's actions reverberate through her relationships and family dynamics. Her affair with Vronsky strains her relationship with Karenin and creates tensions within her immediate and extended family. Tolstoy presents readers with a profound exploration of the consequences of infidelity on individuals and their loved ones, delving into the complexities of familial bonds.

Moral Dilemmas and Choices

The Clash of Desires and Duty

Anna Karenina wrestles with the clash between her personal desires and the duty imposed upon her as a wife and mother. Tolstoy examines the moral dilemmas faced by individuals torn between societal expectations and the pursuit of their own happiness. The novel challenges readers to contemplate the choices individuals make and the moral implications that arise from these decisions.

Anna's Decision to Leave

One of the defining moments in the novel is Anna's decision to leave her husband and son to be with Vronsky. This pivotal choice showcases the lengths individuals will go to pursue their desires and the far-reaching consequences of such decisions. Tolstoy emphasizes the magnitude of these choices and the enduring impact they have on the lives of the characters involved.

The Aftermath of Choices

The consequences of the characters' choices reverberate throughout the novel, shaping their lives and the lives of those around them. Tolstoy explores the aftermath of decisions made in pursuit of love, revealing the complexities of human relationships and the far-reaching consequences of individual actions. The novel serves as a cautionary tale, reminding readers of the enduring effects of choices made in the pursuit of personal happiness.

Love, Loss, and Redemption

Tragic Endings

"Anna Karenina" confronts readers with the tragic consequences that accompany forbidden love. The novel's conclusion is marked by heartbreak, highlighting the devastating toll of societal judgment, guilt, and internal struggles. Tolstoy's exploration of tragic endings elicits a deep emotional response from readers, leaving a lasting impact long after the final pages.

Levin and Kitty's Love Story

Amidst the turmoil of Anna and Vronsky's ill-fated love, Tolstoy interweaves the love story of Levin and Kitty. Their relationship offers a stark contrast to the tragic tale of Anna and Vronsky, presenting a glimmer of hope and redemption. Levin and Kitty's love blossoms amidst sincerity and mutual understanding, showcasing a different path to fulfillment and happiness.

Reflections on Love and Life

"Anna Karenina" serves as a poignant reflection on the nature of love, life, and the consequences of human choices. Tolstoy prompts readers to contemplate the complexities of love and the myriad ways it shapes individuals' lives. The novel offers profound insights into the human condition, provoking introspection and inviting readers to reevaluate their own understanding of love, relationships, and the consequences that arise from following one's desires.

Conclusion

In Leo Tolstoy's "Anna Karenina," love and its consequences take center stage. The novel weaves a captivating tale of forbidden passion, societal expectations, and the enduring impact of personal choices. Through the multifaceted character of Anna Karenina and the moral dilemmas faced by the characters, Tolstoy crafts a narrative that explores the depths of human emotions and the profound repercussions of pursuing love against societal norms. "Anna Karenina" continues to captivate readers with its timeless exploration of love's complexities, reminding us of the enduring consequences of our choices.

Chapter 7: The Great Gatsby

Love, Obsession, and Illusion

The Great Gatsby, written by F. Scott Fitzgerald, is a timeless classic that delves into the complexities of love, obsession, and illusion. Set in the 1920s, the novel explores the glittering but deceptive world of the wealthy elite in America, showcasing the power and destructive nature of these intertwined themes.

"The Great Gatsby" stands as a masterpiece in American literature, captivating readers with its rich character development, intricate storytelling, and exploration of the human condition.

In the Jazz Age's glistening haze,
"The Great Gatsby" paints a complex maze,
Where love, obsession, and illusion collide,
In F. Scott Fitzgerald's timeless ride.
Jay Gatsby, a man self-made,
Obsessed with love, a longing cascade,
His heart entangled in Daisy's snare,
A love affair doomed, caught in a dare.
Obsession grips Gatsby's soul,
Wealth and status, his ultimate goal,
But illusions shroud his pursuit of dreams,
A mirage of happiness, or so it seems.
The American Dream, an elusive prize,
An illusion that fades before our eyes,
Beneath the surface, empty and hollow,
An unattainable dream we all follow.
The upper class, a facade they maintain,
A mask of wealth, hiding disdain,

But beneath their opulence and charm,
Lies moral decay and emotional harm.
Love, obsession, and illusion's grip,
A destructive force, their lives it rips,
Tragedy befalls the characters entwined,
Betrayal, deceit, lives left behind.
In pursuit of desires, they pay the price,
Lost in a world of glitter and vice,
"The Great Gatsby" warns of the cost,
When love, obsession, and illusion are lost.
Through Fitzgerald's words, we come to see,
The human condition's complexity,
And as we close this timeless book,
We ponder the choices we overlook.
For in our own lives, may we be aware,
Of love, obsession, and illusions' snare,
To navigate the illusions we face,
And find true meaning, love's rightful place.

The Great Gatsby: A Brief Overview

Before diving into the themes, let's provide a brief overview of the novel. Set in the Roaring Twenties, "The Great Gatsby" follows the story of Jay Gatsby, a self-made millionaire, and his obsession with Daisy Buchanan, a married woman from his past. As the narrative unfolds, the novel examines the consequences of their ill-fated love affair amidst the backdrop of the jazz age and the pursuit of the elusive American Dream.

Love in "The Great Gatsby"

Love serves as a central theme in "The Great Gatsby," exploring both its power and limitations. At its core, the novel presents the love story between Jay Gatsby and Daisy Buchanan, two characters deeply entwined in a web of longing and desire.

The love between Jay Gatsby and Daisy Buchanan

Gatsby's love for Daisy is all-consuming, fueled by his memories of their past relationship and the belief that he can reclaim their lost connection. Daisy, on the other hand, is torn between her love for Gatsby and the security of her marriage to Tom Buchanan. Their love is hindered by societal expectations, class differences, and the influence of money.

Obsession and illusion in their relationship

Gatsby's love for Daisy borders on obsession, as he becomes consumed by the idea of winning her back. He meticulously constructs an illusion of wealth and success to impress Daisy, believing that material possessions can bridge the gap between them. However, this obsession ultimately blinds Gatsby to the reality of Daisy's character and their incompatible futures.

The impact of societal expectations on their love

"The Great Gatsby" also sheds light on the impact of societal expectations on love. Daisy is torn between the allure of Gatsby's love and the expectations placed upon her as a member of the upper class. The novel highlights the shallowness and superficiality of the social elite, where love often takes a backseat to appearances and reputation.

Obsession in "The Great Gatsby"

Obsession is a pervasive theme throughout the novel, illustrating the lengths individuals will go to attain their desires. Jay Gatsby's obsession lies in his relentless pursuit of wealth, status, and the idealized version of love he associates with Daisy.

Gatsby's obsession with wealth and status

Gatsby's transformation from a poor young man to a millionaire magnate is fueled by his obsession with wealth and the belief that it will bring him happiness and fulfillment. His opulent mansion, extravagant parties, and flashy possessions are all carefully constructed to impress others, particularly Daisy.

The pursuit of the American Dream

Gatsby's obsession with wealth is also rooted in his pursuit of the American Dream, the belief that anyone can achieve success through hard work and determination. He sees wealth as a means to erase his humble origins and win Daisy's heart. However, the novel questions the true attainability and emptiness of this dream.

The consequences of Gatsby's obsession

Gatsby's obsession ultimately leads to his downfall. His relentless pursuit of Daisy blinds him to the reality of their relationship and his own self-destructive actions. Gatsby becomes trapped in a cycle of deception and illusion, which ultimately results in tragedy.

Illusion in "The Great Gatsby"

Illusion, both personal and societal, permeates the world of "The Great Gatsby." The characters are constantly striving to maintain facades, concealing their true selves beneath layers of deception and false appearances.

The illusion of the American Dream

One of the prominent illusions in the novel is the American Dream itself. The characters, including Gatsby, believe that material success and social status will bring them happiness and fulfillment. However, Fitzgerald exposes the hollowness and unattainable nature of this dream, highlighting the disillusionment that lies beneath its glittering surface.

The facade of the wealthy upper class

The wealthy elite in "The Great Gatsby" maintain an illusion of perfection and privilege. They project an image of prosperity, luxury, and sophistication, but beneath the surface lies a world of moral decay, infidelity, and emotional emptiness. The novel reveals the stark contrast between appearances and reality.

The emptiness and disillusionment behind the illusion

"The Great Gatsby" explores the emptiness and disillusionment that lie behind the illusions constructed by the characters. Gatsby's opulent parties, Daisy's superficiality, and the reckless behavior of the upper class all mask deeper feelings of dissatisfaction and unfulfilled desires. The novel serves as a cautionary tale, warning against the dangers of pursuing superficial ideals and illusions.

The destructive power of love, obsession, and illusion

The themes of love, obsession, and illusion intertwine to create a destructive force in "The Great Gatsby." The characters' lives are tragically affected by their entanglement in these complex webs.

Characters' tragic fates

The novel presents a series of tragic fates for its characters. Gatsby's relentless pursuit of Daisy leads to his demise, Tom and Daisy's marriage crumbles under the weight of their infidelity, and Myrtle Wilson pays the ultimate price for her involvement with the upper class. These tragedies serve as a stark reminder of the destructive power of love, obsession, and illusion.

Themes of betrayal, deceit, and tragedy

Betrayal, deceit, and tragedy are recurring themes in "The Great Gatsby." The characters' obsession with their desires leads them to make morally questionable choices, resulting in broken relationships, shattered dreams, and untimely deaths. Fitzgerald explores the consequences of pursuing personal desires at the expense of others, ultimately leading to a sense of tragedy and loss.

Conclusion

"The Great Gatsby" is a timeless novel that explores the themes of love, obsession, and illusion with remarkable depth and complexity. Fitzgerald's portrayal of these intertwined themes serves as a critique of the superficiality and emptiness of the Jazz Age. The novel's enduring relevance lies in its exploration of the human condition and the destructive power of misplaced desires.

Chapter 8: Gone with the Wind

Love in the Face of Turmoil

Love is a powerful force that transcends boundaries and withstands the tests of time. It has the remarkable ability to endure even in the face of turmoil and adversity.

In the face of turmoil, love will stand,
A force unwavering, hand in hand,
It transcends boundaries, knows no bounds,
In its embrace, solace is found.
Challenges arise, testing its might,
Yet love perseveres, shining bright,
Communication, the key to mend,
Obstacles faced, together we'll transcend.
Resilience blooms amidst the strife,
Love's foundation strengthened, giving life,
It heals, it nurtures, a balm for the soul,
Through love, broken pieces can be made whole.
Trust, the anchor that holds us tight,
In turbulent seas, it guides us right,
With honesty and reliability,
We rebuild trust, forging unity.
Love's happiness, a gift to share,
In joyful moments, it's always there,
Through cherished memories and laughter's gleam,
Love illuminates life's turbulent stream.
Kindness, affection, the flames we tend,
Keeping love alive, a commitment we send,
For love's growth and vibrance to sustain,

We prioritize, in devotion's domain.
Personal growth, love's profound gift,
It teaches, challenges, spirits lift,
Empathy, patience, virtues embraced,
Through love's journey, we're truly graced.
Triumphantly, love conquers all,
In the face of turmoil, it won't fall,
A testament to resilience and hope,
Love's unwavering strength helps us cope.
So let us cherish love, embrace its might,
In times of turmoil, it'll be our light,
With open hearts and steadfast will,
Love guides us, even through the stormiest chill.

Love, in all its forms, serves as a guiding light during the darkest of times. Whether it's the love between romantic partners, family members, or friends, it has the potential to provide solace and strength. But what happens when love encounters challenges?

How does it navigate through the turbulent waters of life?

Let's explore.

Understanding Love

Love is a multifaceted emotion that encompasses care, affection, and deep attachment. It is a profound connection between individuals that goes beyond superficial boundaries. Love brings people together, fosters empathy, and ignites a sense of belonging.

Love Amidst Turmoil

Turmoil often arises unexpectedly, testing the strength of any relationship. Whether it's financial difficulties, health crises, or external factors such as societal unrest, love can face immense strain. However, it is during these times that the true power of love becomes evident.

Challenges in Love

Love is not immune to challenges. Communication breakdowns, differences in values, and conflicting expectations can create obstacles in relationships. Moreover, external factors such as career demands and geographical distances can further complicate matters. It is essential to acknowledge these challenges and work towards finding solutions together.

Overcoming Obstacles

Resilience plays a crucial role in overcoming the obstacles that love encounters. It requires a commitment to growth, adaptability, and open communication. By addressing issues head-on, seeking compromise, and providing unwavering support, couples can navigate through even the most trying circumstances.

The Power of Resilience

Resilience allows love to endure and evolve. It enables couples to bounce back from setbacks, learn from their experiences, and build a stronger foundation. Resilience is not about avoiding challenges but rather embracing them as opportunities for growth and transformation.

Love as a Source of Strength

In times of turmoil, love acts as a source of strength. It provides emotional support, stability, and a sense of security. The unwavering presence of love allows individuals to find solace, helping them overcome their fears and face the unknown with courage.

Nurturing Love through Communication

Effective communication is the lifeblood of any relationship. It fosters understanding, resolves conflicts, and strengthens the bond between partners. By actively listening, expressing emotions honestly, and practicing empathy, couples can nurture their love and weather any storm.

Love's Role in Emotional Healing

Love has a remarkable capacity to heal emotional wounds. It offers comfort, acceptance, and a safe space for vulnerability. When individuals face turmoil, love becomes a sanctuary where they can find solace, reassurance, and healing.

Building Trust in Turbulent Times

Trust forms the foundation of any successful relationship. In times of turmoil, trust can be tested and strained. However, by demonstrating honesty, transparency, and reliability, couples can rebuild and strengthen their trust. Trust acts as an anchor, providing stability amidst the storm.

Finding Happiness in Love

Love brings immense joy and happiness into our lives. It allows individuals to share experiences, celebrate victories, and create cherished memories. Even in the face of turmoil, love can be a constant source of happiness, reminding us of the beauty that exists amidst the chaos.

Maintaining Love's Flame

Just as love can endure through tumultuous times, it requires continuous effort to keep its flame alive. Regular acts of kindness, affection, and quality time together are essential in nurturing love. By prioritizing the relationship and staying committed, couples can ensure that their love remains vibrant and resilient.

Love's Impact on Personal Growth

Love has the power to transform individuals and facilitate personal growth. Through love, individuals learn empathy, patience, and selflessness. It challenges them to become better versions of themselves and fosters personal development.

Love's Triumph in the Face of Turmoil

Despite the trials and tribulations that life presents, love has the capacity to triumph. It defies the odds, strengthens bonds, and creates a sense of purpose. Love, in all its complexities, is a testament to the human spirit's resilience and capacity for hope.

Conclusion

Love is a beacon of light that guides us through the darkest storms. It endures in the face of turmoil, providing solace, strength, and happiness. By nurturing love, communicating openly, and embracing resilience, couples can weather any storm that life brings their way.

Chapter 9: Doctor Zhivago

Love Amidst War and Revolution

"Doctor Zhivago" is a renowned novel written by Boris Pasternak, first published in 1957. It is set against the backdrop of war and revolution in Russia during the early 20th century. This epic love story captures the complexities of human emotions and the struggle to find love, happiness, and meaning in a tumultuous and rapidly changing world.

In the realm of words, a tale unfolds,
"Doctor Zhivago," a story that molds,
A world of war and revolution's fire,
Love's struggle, yearning, and desire.
Boris Pasternak, the master behind,
Crafted a novel that forever will bind,
Themes of love, politics, identity's quest,
A tumultuous era, put to the test.
Amidst Russian Revolution's thunderous cries,
And World War's anguish, where hope dies,
Yuri Zhivago, a doctor and poet true,
Finds love's labyrinth, his heart in two.
Lara Antipova, a woman untamed,
Entwined with Yuri, passions unchained,
Their love forbidden, a flame ablaze,
Escaping realities in clandestine ways.
Love, betrayal, sacrifice entwined,
In Pasternak's tale, their paths defined,
The refuge of love, against chaos it strives,
Betrayal's burden, love's sacrifices thrive.

Soviet regime's grip, an iron fist,
Pasternak's critique, in his words insist,
The dehumanizing plight, loss of free will,
A powerful commentary, society's ill.
Controversy and censorship it faced,
Yet Nobel's laurel, its triumph embraced,
A legacy profound, in Russian lore,
"Doctor Zhivago," forevermore.
Love's resilience, amidst turmoil's sway,
A testament to the human spirit's way,
In the darkest hours, love's light still gleams,
"Doctor Zhivago," forever it redeems.
Through pages penned, a masterpiece thrives,
In Boris Pasternak's words, love survives,
A tale immortal, its message profound,
Love's enduring power, forever renowned.

Background on "Doctor Zhivago"

Boris Pasternak, a Russian poet and writer, penned "Doctor Zhivago" during the 1940s and 1950s. The novel explores the themes of love, politics, and the individual's search for identity and purpose. Initially, the Soviet authorities banned its publication due to its critical portrayal of the Communist regime and its nonconformity to socialist realism.

Setting: War and Revolution in Russia

The events of "Doctor Zhivago" unfold in the context of two major historical events: the Russian Revolution of 1917 and World War I. The Russian Revolution marked a period of political and social upheaval, leading to the fall of the Tsarist regime and the rise of the Soviet Union. Simultaneously, World War I ravaged Europe, causing immense suffering and loss of life.

The Love Story of Yuri Zhivago and Lara Antipova

The heart of "Doctor Zhivago" lies in the poignant love story between the protagonist, Yuri Zhivago, and Lara Antipova. Yuri, a doctor and poet, struggles to balance his personal and professional life amidst the chaos of war and revolution. Lara, a young woman with her own trials and tribulations, becomes entangled in Yuri's life, leading to a passionate and forbidden romance.

Yuri Zhivago is torn between his love for his wife, Tonya, and his profound connection with Lara. Their relationship serves as an escape from the harsh realities of their surroundings, offering solace and hope in a time of despair.

Themes of Love, Betrayal, and Sacrifice

"Doctor Zhivago" delves deep into the themes of love, betrayal, and sacrifice. Love serves as a refuge from the brutality and unpredictability of war and revolution. It becomes a driving force for Yuri and Lara, compelling them to defy societal norms and embrace their desires.

Betrayal also plays a significant role in the story, as characters navigate the conflicting expectations and pressures of society. The characters are forced to make difficult choices, often at the expense of their own happiness and the well-being of those around them.

Sacrifice emerges as a recurring motif, with characters making selfless decisions for the greater good. They endure personal hardships and relinquish their own desires in service of their ideals and the welfare of others.

Historical Context and Political Critique

"Doctor Zhivago" provides a scathing critique of the Soviet regime and its impact on individuals and society. Pasternak portrays the devastating consequences of war and revolution, highlighting the loss of personal freedoms and the erosion of basic human rights.

Through the characters' experiences, Pasternak sheds light on the dehumanizing effects of the Communist regime, exposing its flaws and the inherent contradictions within the system. The novel serves as a powerful commentary on the struggle between individual freedom and the oppressive machinery of the state.

Reception and Legacy of "Doctor Zhivago"

Upon its publication, "Doctor Zhivago" faced controversy and censorship in the Soviet Union. However, it gained international recognition, winning the Nobel Prize in Literature in 1958. The novel's profound impact on Russian literature and culture cannot be overstated. It inspired subsequent generations of writers and continues to be celebrated for its rich portrayal of love, resilience, and the human spirit.

Conclusion

"Doctor Zhivago" remains an enduring masterpiece that captures the essence of love amidst war and revolution. Boris Pasternak's remarkable storytelling weaves together personal relationships, political turmoil, and profound themes, inviting readers to reflect on the enduring power of love, even in the darkest of times.

Chapter 10: The Notebook

Enduring Love and Memory

"The Notebook" is a heartwarming and poignant tale that explores the enduring nature of love and the profound impact of memories. Penned by Nicholas Sparks, this beloved novel tells the story of Noah and Allie, two individuals whose love stands the test of time, even in the face of great challenges. At the heart of this captivating narrative lies a notebook, serving as a powerful symbol of their enduring love and the memories they hold dear.

In the realm of ink, a story unfolds,
"The Notebook," a tale of love it holds,
Nicholas Sparks, the masterful weaver,
Crafts a narrative that our hearts endeavor.
Love's Power Unveiled
At the core of this captivating lore,
Love's essence lingers, forevermore,
Noah and Allie's love, unyielding and strong,
Defying odds, transcending time's long song.
Memory's Role, Profound and Deep
Memories, like threads, intricately creep,
Shaping identities, forging paths anew,
In the tapestry of lives, cherished and true.
The joys and pains that memories bring,
In "The Notebook," their significance sings.
The Symbol, Notebook's Pages Wrought
Within its lines, love's story is caught,
Noah's devotion, written with care,
Preserving their love, beyond time's snare.

A symbol of words' enduring might,
The notebook shines, love's eternal light.
Love, Timeless and Unfettered
A love that endures, forever tethered,
Noah and Allie's bond, steadfast and strong,
Through ages, their hearts forever belong.
In a world fleeting, where moments dissolve,
Their love stands firm, evolving and resolve.
Alzheimer's Shadow, Love's Test
Alzheimer's cruel touch, a painful crest,
Straining memories, challenging their love,
Yet, their connection persists, carried above.
A reminder to cherish every precious hour,
To hold dear each memory, like a fragile flower.
Sacrifice and Commitment's Weave
In the face of challenges, love they cleave,
Noah and Allie, guided by their hearts' call,
Embracing sacrifice, commitment standing tall.
Their love's resilience, a beacon of light,
Through sacrifices made, love takes flight.
An Emotional Odyssey Unveiled
An emotional odyssey, their hearts unveiled,
Noah and Allie, evolving, their souls regaled,
Their journey of growth, of lessons learned,
In each other's arms, solace is earned.
Their joys and sorrows, we feel them too,
Through their emotional voyage, our hearts break through.
Setting's Influence, a World Enthralled
The house, the lake, where their love enthralls,
Symbols of their emotions, an intricate dance,
The house, their foundation, their love's expanse.
The lake, mirroring their relationship's tide,

Through the setting's embrace, their love abides.
Film's Impact, Hearts Enraptured
From page to screen, their love captured,
"The Notebook" on film, emotions unfurled,
Deepening the story, in hearts it's twirled.
An indelible mark on culture's embrace,
The film's success, love's universal space.
"The Notebook's" Enduring Allure
Years pass, yet its allure holds sure,
Love, memory, sacrifice, commitment's plea,
Themes timeless, captivating you and me.
"The Notebook" lingers in hearts' embrace,
A testament to love's transformative grace.
In the realm of words, "The Notebook" stands,
A tale of love, crafted by gifted hands,
Nicholas Sparks, his story forever told,
Love's enduring power, a beauty to behold.

The Power of Love

Love is the central theme that drives the narrative of "The Notebook." It is a force that transcends time, defying societal norms and conquering all obstacles. The story beautifully portrays the strength of love, reminding us of its ability to transform lives and inspire hope. Noah and Allie's love is a testament to the power of genuine connections that can withstand the trials and tribulations of life.

The Role of Memory

Memory plays a pivotal role in "The Notebook," weaving together the fabric of the characters' lives. Memories shape their identities, influence their decisions, and ultimately define their relationships. The novel explores how memories can both bring joy and cause pain, as Noah and Allie navigate the complexities of their shared past. It highlights the importance of cherishing and preserving memories, as they become a lifeline to the past when the present becomes uncertain.

The Notebook as a Symbol

The notebook itself is a potent symbol in the story. It represents Noah's unwavering love for Allie and his commitment to keeping their memories alive. Within its pages lie their shared experiences, dreams, and aspirations. The notebook serves as a tangible representation of their love story, immortalizing their connection for generations to come. It symbolizes the power of the written word and the significance of preserving cherished memories.

Love Transcending Time

"The Notebook" showcases a love that transcends time, challenging the boundaries imposed by age and circumstance. Noah and Allie's love story unfolds over several decades, revealing a bond that remains unbreakable despite the passage of time. Their unwavering commitment to one another inspires us to believe in the possibility of lasting love, even in a world that often seems fleeting and ephemeral.

The Impact of Alzheimer's Disease

Alzheimer's disease casts a shadow over Noah and Allie's relationship, testing the strength of their love and memories. The story portrays the devastating effects of the disease on their lives and the challenges it presents in maintaining a connection built on shared memories. Alzheimer's serves as a poignant reminder of the fragility of our recollections and the importance of treasuring every moment we have with our loved ones.

Themes of Sacrifice and Commitment

Sacrifice and commitment are recurring themes in "The Notebook." Noah and Allie face numerous obstacles that demand difficult choices. Their love requires them to make sacrifices and embrace commitment, even when it seems daunting. The novel explores the depth of their devotion and the profound impact of the choices they make in the name of love.

The Emotional Journey of the Characters

Noah and Allie embark on an emotional journey throughout the story. They experience personal growth, learn from their mistakes, and find solace in each other's arms. Their journey is a testament to the resilience of the human spirit and the transformative power of love. As readers, we are captivated by their emotional evolution, empathizing with their joys and sorrows.

The Influence of Setting

The setting of "The Notebook" plays a vital role in shaping the story. The house Noah renovates and the picturesque lake become integral parts of the narrative, reflecting the characters' emotions and experiences. The house symbolizes the foundation of their love, while the lake represents the ebb and flow of their relationship. The carefully crafted setting enhances the themes of love and memory, immersing readers in a world where every detail holds significance.

The Impact of the Film Adaptation

"The Notebook" gained even greater prominence with its film adaptation, captivating audiences worldwide. The movie brought the characters to life and further intensified the emotional resonance of the story. It left an indelible mark on popular culture, propelling the novel to even greater acclaim. The film's success attests to the universal appeal of enduring love and the enduring legacy of "The Notebook."

The Enduring Popularity of "The Notebook"

Years after its publication, "The Notebook" continues to captivate readers around the globe. Its timeless themes of love, memory, sacrifice, and commitment resonate with people from all walks of life. The enduring popularity of the novel speaks to its ability to touch hearts, reminding us of the power of love to transform lives and transcend the boundaries of time.

Conclusion

"The Notebook" is a remarkable tale that weaves together the threads of enduring love and treasured memories. Through the power of Noah and Allie's story, Nicholas Sparks reminds us of the profound impact love and memory can have on our lives. It serves as a poignant reminder to cherish our connections, preserve our memories, and believe in the enduring power of love.

Chapter 11: Bridget Jones's Diary

Love and Self-Discovery

Bridget Jones's Diary, both a bestselling novel by Helen Fielding and a successful film adaptation, explores the journey of a witty, relatable woman named Bridget Jones as she navigates the complexities of love, relationships, and self-discovery. With a blend of humor, romance, and a strong dose of reality, the story captivates audiences and provides valuable insights into the human experience.

In the world of ink, a tale unfolds,
"Bridget Jones's Diary" we eagerly behold,
Helen Fielding's creation, a woman's quest,
Love, self-discovery, humor at its best.
Bridget's Search for Love, A Relatable Tale,
In her thirties, she sets out to prevail,
Navigating the challenges, hopes, and fears,
Her journey resonates, shedding laughter and tears.
Mark Darcy or Daniel Cleaver, A Dilemma So,
Two paths diverge, where should she go?
Mark, the steady choice, reliable and true,
Daniel, the charmer, sparks something new.
Self-Worth and Empowerment, Lessons Learned,
Bridget blossoms, her inner fire earned,
Beyond judgments and societal norms,
She finds her value, her spirit transforms.
Self-Acceptance, Bridget's Path of Growth,
Insecurities shed, she embraces her both,
Her weight, her career, her sense of belonging,
She learns to love herself, her spirit ever-strong.

Embracing Imperfections, Overcoming Insecurities,
Bridget's journey resonates with simplicities,
Happiness from within, not from external gaze,
A lesson we cherish throughout our days.
Beyond Romance, Personal Fulfillment Soars,
Career, friendships, hobbies, and more,
Bridget shows us the importance to pursue,
Our passions and dreams, our happiness too.
Humor, a Key Ingredient in the Mix,
Bridget's clumsiness, her comedic fix,
Inner monologues and amusing strife,
Create a narrative that brings laughter to life.
Relatability and Reflection, Comedy's Role,
Through Bridget's wit, we find our own soul,
Escaping reality, pondering our own plight,
Comedy opens doors, both day and night.
Breaking Stereotypes, Comedy's Great Gift,
Bridget defies norms, a paradigm shift,
Authenticity and quirkiness, a woman's right,
Through humor, we challenge, we take flight.
A Cultural Phenomenon, Bridget's Fame,
Pop culture and feminism forever changed,
The story ignited conversations, deep and wide,
Gender roles, representation, with passion it rides.
Inspiring a Generation, Bridget's Impact,
Her journey empowers, her character intact,
Embracing imperfections, navigating with pride,
Women find strength, alongside Bridget they stride.
In the realm of ink, "Bridget Jones's Diary" thrives,
A tale of love, self-discovery, and humorous lives,
Its impact, far-reaching, feminist discourse unfolds,
As Bridget inspires, a beacon for all to behold.

Bridget's Quest for Love

Bridget Jones's Diary revolves around Bridget's perpetual search for love and companionship. As a single woman in her thirties, Bridget encounters the challenges of finding the right partner in a world filled with societal expectations and self-doubt. Her relatable experiences resonate with readers and viewers alike, who empathize with the universal desire for love and acceptance.

The Dilemma of Choosing Between Mark Darcy and Daniel Cleaver

One of the central conflicts in Bridget's romantic journey is the choice between Mark Darcy and Daniel Cleaver. Mark, a reserved and seemingly uptight lawyer, represents stability and sincerity, while Daniel, her charming and flirtatious boss, represents excitement and spontaneity. Bridget's struggle to make this decision reflects the dilemmas faced by many individuals when choosing between the safe option and the allure of the unknown.

Lessons in Self-Worth and Empowerment

Throughout her journey, Bridget learns valuable lessons about self-worth and empowerment. As she navigates the complexities of romantic relationships, she gradually discovers her own value beyond societal expectations and superficial judgments. Bridget's growth serves as an inspiration for readers and viewers to embrace their imperfections, celebrate their uniqueness, and demand respect and equality in their own lives.

Bridget's Journey Towards Self-Acceptance

"Bridget Jones's Diary" highlights the importance of self-acceptance and personal growth. Bridget struggles with insecurities about her weight, career, and overall sense of belonging. However, as the story unfolds, she learns to overcome these insecurities and embrace herself fully. This journey resonates with audiences who have experienced similar struggles, fostering a sense of connection and encouraging them to embark on their path of self-discovery.

Overcoming Insecurities and Embracing Imperfections

Bridget's journey is marked by her ability to overcome insecurities and embrace her imperfections. As she becomes more self-aware and self-accepting, she realizes that true happiness comes from within, not from conforming to societal norms or seeking validation from others. This message resonates with readers and viewers, reminding them to value their unique qualities and focus on personal growth.

Pursuit of Personal Fulfillment

In addition to romantic relationships, "Bridget Jones's Diary" emphasizes the importance of personal fulfillment. Bridget's experiences in her career, friendships, and hobbies contribute to her growth and happiness. By prioritizing her own aspirations and desires, she demonstrates the significance of self-discovery and the pursuit of personal fulfillment outside of traditional relationship dynamics.

The Role of Humor in "Bridget Jones's Diary"

Humor plays a vital role in "Bridget Jones's Diary," adding depth and relatability to the story. Bridget's endearing clumsiness, her humorous inner monologues, and the amusing situations she finds herself in create a light-hearted and enjoyable narrative.

Comedy as a Vehicle for Relatability and Reflection

The comedic elements in the story make Bridget relatable to a wide range of readers and viewers. Her mishaps and humorous observations about everyday life provide an escape from reality while inviting introspection. The humor becomes a vehicle for both entertainment and reflection, allowing the audience to see their own experiences through Bridget's witty perspective.

Breaking Stereotypes through Humor

"Bridget Jones's Diary" challenges stereotypes and societal expectations through humor. Bridget's character defies traditional notions of the "perfect" woman, embracing her flaws and quirks. The comedy in the story breaks down barriers, encouraging individuals to be authentic and challenge societal norms that restrict personal growth and self-expression.

Bridget Jones's Diary: A Cultural Phenomenon

Beyond its entertainment value, "Bridget Jones's Diary" has had a significant impact on pop culture and feminist discourse. The story and its protagonist have become icons in their own right, inspiring a generation of women to embrace their individuality and demand equality.

Impact on Pop Culture and Feminist Discourse

"Bridget Jones's Diary" sparked conversations about gender roles, societal expectations, and the importance of female representation in media. The story's success prompted further exploration of complex female characters in literature and film, contributing to the broader feminist movement and paving the way for more inclusive narratives.

Inspiring a Generation of Women

The relatability and authenticity of Bridget Jones resonated deeply with women worldwide. Her journey of love, self-discovery, and empowerment became a source of inspiration and empowerment for many, encouraging them to embrace their imperfections, navigate relationships with confidence, and pursue their personal and professional goals.

Conclusion

"Bridget Jones's Diary" is more than just a romantic comedy; it is a story that explores the universal themes of love, self-discovery, and the power of humor. Through Bridget's relatable experiences, the narrative captures the complexities of relationships and the importance of personal growth and acceptance. The impact of this cultural phenomenon reaches far beyond the pages and screens, inspiring individuals to embrace their own journeys of love and self-discovery.

Chapter 12: Twilight

Love and Fantasy

Twilight is a captivating series of novels that have taken the world by storm. With its unique blend of romance and fantasy, the Twilight saga has captured the hearts of millions of readers worldwide.

In the realm of twilight's soft embrace,
A saga unfolds, captivating with grace,
Stephenie Meyer's creation, a world so grand,
Where romance and fantasy entwine hand in hand.
Vampires Reimagined, a New Light Shines,
No longer monstrous, their love defines,
Supernatural beings with powers untold,
Thirsting not for blood, but for a love to behold.
Bella and Edward, Love's Intensity,
A human and vampire, a forbidden decree,
Their hearts entwined, against all odds they fight,
A love that ignites, casting shadows into the night.
Soulmates, Destined to Forever Be,
Bella and Edward, bound eternally,
Their connection profound, an unbreakable thread,
In a world where true love is often misread.
A Triangle of Love, Choices to Make,
Jacob enters the fray, hearts at stake,
A werewolf's love, vying for Bella's heart,
A tumultuous path, tearing them apart.
Fantasy Unveiled, Twilight's Charm,
A world where supernatural beings swarm,
Vampires, werewolves, a realm so surreal,

A tapestry of wonder, where dreams congeal.
World-Building Magic, Immersive Delight,
In Forks, Washington, a world takes flight,
Detailed and vivid, its essence so grand,
A universe crafted by a masterful hand.
Supernatural Allure, Temptation Unleashed,
Extraordinary powers, by creatures reached,
Enthralling readers, a sense of wonder bestowed,
Within this realm, where fantasies are sowed.
Escape to Another Reality, Twilight's Gift,
A respite from the ordinary, a much-needed lift,
In romance and adventure, danger's embrace,
A refuge where emotions find their rightful place.
Twilight's Impact, a Cultural Blaze,
A phenomenon that continues to amaze,
Films, merchandise, a devoted fandom's delight,
Its presence etched forever in popular culture's sight.
Empowered Characters, Breaking the Mold,
Bella's strength and resilience, a story to behold,
Challenging norms, inspiring young minds,
The power of female protagonists, a legacy that binds.
In the twilight's glow, a tale so profound,
Twilight enchants, its allure unbound,
With its captivating love and fantasy's sway,
A journey awaits, where hearts and dreams may play.

Understanding Twilight

The Twilight Saga The Twilight Saga, written by Stephenie Meyer, is a series of four novels: Twilight, New Moon, Eclipse, and Breaking Dawn. Set in the town of Forks, Washington, the series follows the life of Isabella Swan, or Bella, as she navigates the complexities of love and the supernatural.

The Magic of Vampires One of the key elements that sets Twilight apart is its portrayal of vampires. Unlike traditional depictions of vampires as bloodthirsty monsters, the vampires in Twilight possess a unique blend of supernatural abilities and an undying thirst for love. This fresh take on vampires adds an intriguing layer to the story.

Love in Twilight

Bella and Edward's Romance At the heart of the Twilight series is the intense and passionate love story between Bella Swan and Edward Cullen. Their relationship is filled with challenges and obstacles, as Bella is a human and Edward is a vampire. Their forbidden love creates a sense of urgency and excitement that keeps readers hooked.

The Concept of Soulmates Twilight explores the concept of soulmates, portraying Bella and Edward as two souls destined to be together. This notion of a deep, unbreakable connection resonates with readers and taps into their desire for true love and eternal bonds.

The Triangle of Love Adding further complexity to the romantic narrative, Twilight introduces a love triangle between Bella, Edward, and Jacob Black, a werewolf. This triangular dynamic creates tension and conflict, keeping readers engrossed in the series as they wonder who Bella will ultimately choose.

Fantasy in Twilight

Immersive World Building One of the reasons Twilight has gained such a dedicated following is its immersive world-building. The author has created a rich and detailed universe filled with supernatural beings, such as vampires, werewolves, and shape-shifters. This fantastical setting allows readers to escape into a world where anything is possible.

The Appeal of Supernatural The allure of the supernatural is another aspect that draws readers into the Twilight series. The extraordinary abilities and powers possessed by the vampires and werewolves add excitement and intrigue to the story, creating a sense of wonder and fascination.

Escaping into a Different Reality Twilight offers readers a chance to escape from the mundane and enter a realm where romance, adventure, and danger coexist. The series provides an opportunity to indulge in a fantasy world and experience a range of emotions, from heart-pounding excitement to tender moments of love.

Impact of Twilight

Popularity and Cultural Phenomenon Twilight has become a cultural phenomenon, captivating not only readers but also spawning a successful film franchise. The series has amassed a loyal fan base, and its popularity has led to numerous spin-offs and merchandise. Twilight has left an indelible mark on popular culture.

Empowering Female Characters Another significant impact of Twilight is its portrayal of strong and independent female characters. Bella, despite her vulnerability, displays resilience and determination, challenging traditional gender roles. The series has inspired young readers by showcasing the strength of female protagonists.

Conclusion

Twilight is more than just a love story or a fantasy series; it is a cultural phenomenon that has captured the imaginations of millions. With its captivating romance, magical world-building, and empowering characters, Twilight continues to enchant readers worldwide. Whether you're a fan of supernatural romance or simply seeking an escape from reality, Twilight offers a compelling journey into the realms of love and fantasy.

Chapter 13: Fifty Shades of Grey

Exploring the Complexities of Desire

In the realm of literature, certain books manage to capture the attention of millions, becoming cultural phenomena that ignite discussions and spark debates. "Fifty Shades of Grey" by E.L. James is undoubtedly one such book. Published in 2011, this erotic romance novel took the world by storm, intriguing readers with its provocative content and captivating characters.

In the depths of desire's mysterious realm,
"Fifty Shades of Grey" took hold, overwhelming the helm.
E.L. James penned a provocative tale,
Igniting passions, leaving readers enthralled, without fail.
Within its pages, the story unfurled,
Anastasia Steele and Christian Grey's world.
Their unconventional bond, a dance of power,
BDSM's allure, a revelation to devour.
Desire's complexity, it knows no bounds,
Intertwining with love, where passion resounds.
Yet societal norms cast shadows of doubt,
As desires clash, conflicts play out.
Deep in our psyche, desire does reside,
Shaped by experiences, perspectives worldwide.
Unconscious longings, fantasies untold,
Molding desires, as secrets unfold.
Controversy surrounds this tale's embrace,
Critics question its portrayal, seeking to retrace,
BDSM's boundaries, consent's sacred space,
Navigating complexities with grace.

Still, its allure found a massive following,
Exploring hidden desires, seductively beckoning.
Escape from reality, a tantalizing ride,
"Fifty Shades of Grey" gave voices a stride.
Sexual empowerment, a central theme,
Challenging taboos, breaking the mainstream.
Consent and trust, cornerstones of desire,
Initiating dialogues, setting souls afire.
The societal impact, both praised and debated,
Expanded horizons, boundaries sedated.
Conversations ignited, breaking through the veil,
"BDSM" no longer whispered, its truths prevail.
In the end, "Fifty Shades of Grey" reveals,
Desire's labyrinthine path, its power appeals.
A catalyst for change, a story that roared,
Navigating desires, in all their aspects explored.
Through controversy and acclaim, it remains,
A testament to desire's intricacies, no reins.
"Fifty Shades of Grey" pushed boundaries, it's true,
A reminder that desires, in us, all accrue.

Understanding Desire

Desire, in its essence, is a powerful force that drives human behavior. It encompasses a wide range of emotions, from yearning and passion to longing and attraction. As a fundamental aspect of human psychology, desire shapes our relationships, fantasies, and aspirations. It is a force that can both exhilarate and confound us, bringing pleasure and pain in equal measure.

Unveiling "Fifty Shades of Grey"

Before diving into the intricacies of desire, let's take a closer look at "Fifty Shades of Grey" itself. The book follows the unconventional relationship between Anastasia Steele, a young college student, and Christian Grey, a wealthy entrepreneur with a taste for BDSM (bondage, discipline, dominance, submission, sadism, and masochism). The narrative explores the evolving dynamics of their connection, delving into their desires, fears, and vulnerabilities.

The Complexity of Desire

Desire is a complex phenomenon that defies easy categorization. It can intertwine with love, but it can also exist independently. The interplay between desire and emotional intimacy is a nuanced dance, with each influencing the other in profound ways. Additionally, societal norms and expectations shape our desires, often leading to internal conflicts and self-discovery.

Psychological Aspects of Desire

Desire is deeply rooted in our psyche, influenced by our experiences, upbringing, and personal beliefs. Fantasies and imagination play a significant role in shaping our desires, allowing us to explore the forbidden or the unconventional within the realm of our minds. Psychological theories offer insights into the nature of desire, including the role of unconscious desires and the impact of societal conditioning.

Controversies Surrounding "Fifty Shades of Grey"

It is important to acknowledge the controversies that surround "Fifty Shades of Grey." The book has faced criticism for its portrayal of BDSM, with concerns raised about consent, boundaries, and the potential glamorization of abusive relationships. While proponents argue that the book explores consensual kink and sexual liberation, detractors question the accuracy of its representation and express concerns about the influence it may have on readers.

Analyzing the Appeal of "Fifty Shades of Grey"

Despite the controversies, "Fifty Shades of Grey" resonated with millions of readers around the world. The allure of the book lies in its exploration of forbidden desires, tapping into the hidden corners of human longing and curiosity. By giving voice to our most secret fantasies, the book offers a sense of escapism and titillation that captivated audiences and ignited conversations about sexuality and desire.

Understanding Sexual Empowerment

"Fifty Shades of Grey" contributed to discussions around sexual empowerment, challenging societal taboos and encouraging individuals to explore their desires without shame. It highlighted the importance of consent, communication, and trust in relationships, while also raising questions about the boundaries between pleasure and pain. The concept of sexual empowerment became a focal point in contemporary dialogues about sexuality and personal autonomy.

Societal Impact of "Fifty Shades of Grey"

The influence of "Fifty Shades of Grey" extends beyond the realm of literature. The book sparked a broader cultural conversation about desire and sexuality, challenging traditional norms and fostering a more open dialogue about previously taboo subjects. It propelled BDSM into the mainstream, leading to an increased awareness and understanding of alternative sexual practices. However, it also drew criticism for potentially reinforcing harmful stereotypes and misconceptions.

Conclusion

"Fifty Shades of Grey" serves as a testament to the intricacies of desire and its impact on human relationships. The book explores the fine line between passion and obsession, consent and control, and challenges conventional notions of love and intimacy. While the controversies surrounding it are valid, "Fifty Shades of Grey" undeniably opened doors for conversations about desire, sexual empowerment, and the diverse nature of human longing.

Chapter 14: Me Before You

Love and Sacrifice

Love and sacrifice are intertwined in the intricate fabric of relationships. It is through the act of sacrificing that love can transcend the boundaries of self-interest and reach new heights. In the bestselling novel "Me Before You" by Jojo Moyes, the themes of love and sacrifice take center stage, portraying the profound impact these elements can have on individuals and their relationships.

Love's embrace, entwined with sacrifice's grace,
In relationships, a dance they fervently trace.
For in the act of giving, selflessly,
Love transcends, reaching heights unseen.
Sacrifice, a treasure bestowed with care,
A gift of self, willingly shared.
Emotional, physical, and financial alike,
Its forms diverse, love's essence to strike.
In the novel "Me Before You," we find,
A tapestry of love and sacrifice entwined.
Louisa Clark, with heart pure and bold,
Devotes herself, sacrifices untold.
Her aspirations on hold, her life set aside,
Louisa tends to Will, a love amplified.
She tends to his needs, both physical and deep,
Creating a haven of love, where spirits leap.
And Will, though bound by tragedy's hand,
Sacrifices his own, for Louisa's dreams to expand.
Encouraging growth, her potential to embrace,
A love so profound, even through space.

Sacrifice, a measure of love's grandeur,
An expression of care, a bond to ensure.
Yet, limits exist, a delicate art,
Balance between selflessness and one's own heart.
Communication, key in this intricate dance,
Understanding desires, boundaries enhanced.
Recognition of sacrifices, gratitude's embrace,
Strengthens the bond, love's eternal grace.
In real-life relationships, sacrifice abounds,
Supporting careers, accommodating life's rounds.
Clear communication, appreciation's song,
Fostering a love that remains lifelong.
Love and sacrifice, harmonious duet,
A foundation to build a relationship set.
Where needs are expressed, boundaries understood,
A union that thrives with shared goals for good.
In the realm of love, sacrifice is revered,
A testament to care, devotion adhered.
"Me Before You" reminds us, in words so true,
That love and sacrifice create a love anew.
So let us embrace love's sacrificial art,
With open hearts, let compassion impart.
For in the act of giving, we truly find,
Love's transformative power, gentle and kind.

Understanding Sacrifice in Relationships

The Concept of Sacrifice

Sacrifice, in the context of relationships, refers to willingly giving up something of value for the benefit or well-being of another person. It involves selflessness, empathy, and a genuine desire to contribute to the happiness of a loved one. Sacrifice can manifest in various forms, from small everyday gestures to more significant life-altering choices.

Types of Sacrifice in Relationships

Sacrifice in relationships can take on diverse forms, such as emotional, physical, or financial sacrifices. Emotional sacrifices may include putting aside personal desires to support a partner's dreams or providing a listening ear during difficult times. Physical sacrifices might involve adjusting one's lifestyle or routines to accommodate a partner's needs or preferences. Financial sacrifices could entail making monetary contributions or giving up certain luxuries to secure the well-being of a loved one.

Importance of Sacrifice in Love

Sacrifice plays a crucial role in fostering love and strengthening the bonds between individuals. It demonstrates a willingness to put the needs and happiness of the other person above one's own. Sacrifice can create a sense of trust, security, and reciprocity within a relationship. It signifies dedication, commitment, and a shared journey towards mutual growth and happiness.

Love and Sacrifice in "Me Before You"

Brief Overview of the Novel

"Me Before You" is a poignant love story that follows the lives of Louisa Clark and Will Traynor. Louisa, a cheerful and quirky young woman, becomes a caregiver for Will, a once-vibrant man who is now quadriplegic due to a tragic accident. As Louisa immerses herself in her new role, an unexpected bond forms between her and Will, leading to a complex exploration of love and sacrifice.

Louisa Clark's Sacrifices for Will Traynor

Louisa Clark's character embodies the essence of sacrifice throughout the novel. Initially hired as a caregiver, she selflessly devotes herself to Will's well-being, going above and beyond her duties. Louisa sacrifices her personal aspirations, putting her own life on hold to support and uplift Will's spirits. Her sacrifices range from assisting with his physical care to providing emotional companionship and fostering an environment of love and understanding.

Will Traynor's Sacrifices for Louisa Clark

In "Me Before You," Will Traynor's character also showcases sacrificial acts. Despite his own frustrations and limitations, Will makes sacrifices to ensure Louisa's happiness and personal growth. He encourages her to explore her potential and embrace opportunities that she would have never considered before. Will's sacrifices go beyond his own desires, as he wishes for Louisa to lead a fulfilling life even in his absence.

Sacrifice as a Measure of Love

Sacrifice as an Expression of Care

Sacrifice serves as a profound expression of care and devotion within a relationship. It demonstrates an individual's willingness to prioritize their partner's happiness and well-being above their own desires. Sacrifice can be seen as an active demonstration of love, solidifying the emotional connection between two people.

The Limits of Sacrifice

While sacrifice is an essential aspect of love, it is crucial to recognize its limits. Sacrificing too much without considering one's own needs and well-being can lead to feelings of resentment or imbalance within the relationship. It is essential to strike a balance between selflessness and self-care to maintain a healthy and fulfilling partnership.

Finding Balance in Sacrifice

To strike the right balance, open communication and understanding are paramount. Partners should openly discuss their expectations, desires, and boundaries to ensure that sacrifices are made willingly and without coercion. Recognizing and appreciating each other's sacrifices can help foster a deep sense of gratitude and strengthen the bond between individuals.

Sacrifice in Real-Life Relationships

Examples of Sacrifice in Relationships

In real-life relationships, sacrifice manifests in myriad ways. It could involve supporting a partner's career aspirations by relocating, compromising on personal preferences to accommodate the other person's needs, or making financial sacrifices for the sake of shared goals. These acts of sacrifice contribute to the overall health and longevity of the relationship.

Communicating and Recognizing Sacrifice

It is essential to establish clear channels of communication within a relationship to express needs, desires, and boundaries effectively. By openly discussing sacrifices and their implications, couples can ensure that their acts of sacrifice are understood, appreciated, and reciprocated. Recognizing and acknowledging each other's sacrifices fosters a sense of gratitude and strengthens the emotional connection.

Building a Healthy Relationship with Sacrifice

Sacrifice should not be the sole foundation of a relationship but rather a complementary aspect. It is important to establish a healthy dynamic where both partners feel comfortable expressing their needs and desires. By understanding each other's boundaries and finding compromises, couples can build a relationship that flourishes with love, support, and shared aspirations.

***

Conclusion

LOVE AND SACRIFICE are inseparable elements that shape the dynamics of relationships. "Me Before You" beautifully portrays the power of sacrificial acts in the context of love, highlighting their ability to transform lives and deepen emotional connections. Sacrifice, when approached with balance and open communication, can serve as a profound expression of care and contribute to the growth and longevity of relationships.

Chapter 15: Love through the Ages

A Critical Analysis

Love is a complex and timeless emotion that has fascinated humanity throughout history. From ancient times to the digital age, love stories have played a significant role in shaping our understanding of romantic relationships.

In the realm of love, tales unfold,
Through ages past, their stories told.
From ancient times to present days,
Their impact on our hearts still sways.
In myth and legend, love's fire burns,
Cleopatra's passion, Mark Antony yearns.
Pyramus and Thisbe, a tragic fate,
Love's sacrifice, a timeless trait.
Shakespeare's words, a lover's guide,
"Romeo and Juliet" side by side.
Beatrice and Benedick's witty dance,
In "Much Ado About Nothing," love's advance.
Classic novels paint love's grand design,
"Pride and Prejudice," a love divine.
"Jane Eyre" and "Wuthering Heights" profound,
True love's power, forever renowned.
Hollywood's romance upon the screen,
"Gone with the Wind," a love supreme.
"Casablanca" and "The Notebook" too,
Love's portrayal, captivating and true.
In modern tales, love's varied theme,
"The Fault in Our Stars," love's bittersweet gleam.

"Crazy Rich Asians," love's cultural embrace,
Diverse narratives, love finds its place.
In the digital age, love finds new ways,
Online connections in the virtual haze.
Long-distance relationships take flight,
Love in the digital realm takes its height.
Love's dynamics change with the years,
Gender roles shift, breaking old frontiers.
Equality sought, love's balance found,
In partnership's dance, a harmonious sound.
Yet caution must be heeded, for we see,
Idealized love can bring uncertainty.
Embracing imperfections, love's true art,
Creates foundations strong, from the heart.
Love stories reflect our deepest desire,
To understand ourselves, to aspire.
Across cultures diverse, love finds its voice,
A universal thread, we all rejoice.
Love stories hold a power so grand,
They touch our souls, they make us understand.
They shape our beliefs, our society's quest,
For empathy, acceptance, and love's very best.
As we explore love's timeless grace,
In narratives that leave a lasting trace,
Let us cherish the tales that make us see,
The beauty and complexity of love's decree.
For love, through the ages, will endure,
Its influence profound, its essence pure.
In love stories' embrace, we find our way,
Navigating love's depths, each and every day.

Love through the ages encompasses the collective experiences and narratives of love across different time periods. By delving into the world of famous love stories, we gain insights into the ideals, challenges, and transformations that love has undergone throughout history. In this critical analysis, we will examine how these stories have shaped modern relationships, inspiring individuals and influencing societal perceptions.

Love in Ancient Times

In ancient times, love's tales were told,
In literature and myths of old.
Cleopatra and Antony, a love so grand,
Their passion echoed across the land.
Pyramus and Thisbe, a love undone,
Through the crack in the wall, their hearts as one.
Their tragic fate, a tale of woe,
Love's sacrifice, a bond that would show.
Passion burned bright, in ancient lore,
Love's flames engulfed, forevermore.
Sacrifice and devotion, a timeless theme,
In love's tapestry, a cherished gleam.
Destiny's hand, a guiding force,
In ancient tales, love took its course.
From gods and mortals, a divine affair,
Love's power, beyond compare.
Ancient love stories, a foundation laid,
Ideals of romance, they portrayed.
Passion, sacrifice, destiny's decree,
In ancient times, love set us free.

Love has been a central theme in ancient literature and mythology. From the passionate love affair of Cleopatra and Mark Antony to the tragic tale of Pyramus and Thisbe, ancient love stories have provided a foundation for romantic ideals. These narratives have often explored themes of passion, sacrifice, and destiny, setting the stage for enduring notions of love that continue to resonate with us today.

Shakespearean Love Stories

Shakespeare, the bard of love's delight,
With words that dance and emotions ignite.
In "Romeo and Juliet," a love so bright,
Star-crossed souls, bound by fate's tight.
Their tragic end, a tale of woe,
Love's passion, a fire that did grow.
From feuding houses, love did bloom,
In death they found love's eternal room.
In "Much Ado About Nothing," we see,
Beatrice and Benedick, a banter free.
Their witty words, a playful fight,
Love's hidden flame, shining so bright.
Shakespeare's plays, a tapestry of emotion,
Love's depths explored with fierce devotion.
Tragedy and passion, love's sweet song,
In timeless tales, our hearts belong.
For centuries, his works endure,
Love's essence captured, forever pure.
Shakespearean love stories, a cherished treasure,
In our understanding, they leave a measure.

The works of William Shakespeare have had an indelible impact on the portrayal of love. From the star-crossed lovers in "Romeo and Juliet" to the witty banter of Beatrice and Benedick in "Much Ado About Nothing," Shakespeare's plays have captured the complexity and intensity of human emotions. The timeless themes of love, tragedy, and passion explored in these plays have influenced our understanding of romantic relationships for centuries.

Classic Romantic Novels

In classic novels, love's tale unfurls,

"Pride and Prejudice," love's dance twirls.
Jane Austen's words, a world so fine,
Societal expectations intertwine.
Elizabeth and Darcy, a love's rebirth,
Overcoming pride, finding their worth.
Through misunderstandings and misgivings, they strive,
True love prevails, against all odds, they thrive.
"Jane Eyre," a heroine so strong,
In Brontë's world, love's journey long.
From the depths of Thornfield's mystery,
Jane and Rochester, love's history.
A tale of passion, of secrets kept,
Love's power awakened, hearts accept.
Through trials and fires, they find their way,
Love's flame burns bright, come what may.
And on the moors, "Wuthering Heights" stands,
A tale of love, of wild demands.
Heathcliff and Catherine, a love untamed,
Obsession and longing, their souls inflamed.
Brontë's masterpiece, a dark romance,
Love's turmoil, a fateful chance.
In haunting echoes, love's legacy,
Challenging conventions, setting love free.
Classic romantic novels, timeless art,
They shape our perception, touch the heart.
Societal expectations, love's fierce fight,
Personal growth, love's shining light.
Through pages turned and characters embraced,
Genuine connections, love's truth encased.
In classic romances, we find our way,
Challenging conventions, love's legacy to stay.

CLASSIC ROMANTIC NOVELS like "Pride and Prejudice," "Jane Eyre," and "Wuthering Heights" have become beloved literary masterpieces, shaping our perception of love. These novels explore themes of societal expectations, personal growth, and the power of true love. Through compelling narratives and well-developed characters, they have left an enduring impact on modern relationships, challenging conventions and inspiring individuals to seek genuine connections.

Hollywood Romance Movies

In Hollywood's realm, love's tale is spun,
Where dreams and passions are never undone.
"Gone with the Wind" swept hearts away,
Scarlett and Rhett, love's tempestuous play.
"Casablanca" whispers love's refrain,
Rick and Ilsa, hearts entwined in pain.
A timeless classic, their love's lament,
Amidst war's chaos, a love unbent.
"The Notebook" tells a love so true,
Noah and Allie, a love that grew.
Their story etched in hearts forevermore,
Love's trials faced, their spirits soar.
Hollywood's romance, a grand affair,
Grand gestures, passions beyond compare.
From silver screen, ideals are born,
Influencing how love is adorned.
But let us remember, as we aspire,
That Hollywood's tales may sometimes inspire,
Yet love's reality is ours to create,
In genuine connections, love finds its state.
So cherish the movies, the dreams they bring,
But know that true love, it takes its own wing.
For in our hearts and in our own way,
We shape our love story, day by day.

Hollywood has played a significant role in shaping modern perceptions of love. Iconic romance movies like "Gone with the Wind," "Casablanca," and "The Notebook" have captured the imagination of audiences worldwide. These films often depict grand gestures, passionate romances, and dramatic conflicts, influencing our ideas of love and romance. While they may not always reflect reality, they continue to inspire and entertain, shaping our expectations in relationships.

Love in the Digital Age

In a digital realm where love does thrive,
Connections forged through screens, they come alive.
Online dating, a virtual embrace,
Love's search transformed in this digital space.
Long-distance relationships, love's test,
Through screens and pixels, hearts invest.
Bound by distance, yet love's flame burns,
In virtual worlds, love's lesson learns.
But amidst the screens, a question arises,
Authenticity questioned, trust compromises.
Emotional intimacy, a challenge to find,
In the digital age, love's complexities bind.
Are virtual interactions true and real,
Or masks we wear, emotions concealed?
Love's touch and presence, do they remain,
Or fade away, lost in the digital terrain?
Yet the digital age brings opportunities anew,
Greater connectivity, love's horizons grew.
Love transcends borders, love knows no bounds,
In virtual spaces, love's symphony resounds.
So let us navigate this digital domain,
With caution and care, love's truth sustain.
Seeking genuine connections, hearts in tune,

Amidst the screens, love's blossoms bloom.
For love, though digital, can still be true,
If we nurture it with trust and breakthrough.
In the digital age, love finds its way,
Authentic, meaningful connections stay.

The advent of technology and social media has transformed the landscape of modern relationships. Online dating, virtual connections, and long-distance relationships have become commonplace. The digital age presents both challenges and opportunities for love, with new modes of communication and the potential for greater connectivity. However, it also raises questions about authenticity, emotional intimacy, and the impact of virtual interactions on genuine connections.

The Evolution of Relationship Dynamics

Through pages and screens, love stories told,
Influencing the dynamics that unfold.
Famous tales shaping our ideals above,
Guiding relationships, the power thereof.
Gender roles shifting, breaking free,
Love's evolution, a symphony we see.
As women rise, with agency and might,
Love's portrayal reflects a changing light.
Literature and media, a mirror they hold,
Unveiling the path where equality unfolds.
Power dynamics shifting, seeking balance true,
Love's journey progresses, a path anew.
Understanding these shifts, we navigate,
The complexities of love, we contemplate.
Appreciating progress, the strides we've made,
In achieving partnerships, foundations laid.
Love's evolution, an ever-changing dance,
Breaking molds, giving love a chance.

Embracing diversity, love's tapestry is woven,
With respect and equality, our bonds are proven.
So let us honor the past and embrace the new,
Love's dynamics evolving, as we journey through.
Famous stories guide us, lessons learned,
Love's growth and progress, forever earned.

Famous love stories have not only influenced our ideals of love but also the dynamics of relationships. They have contributed to changing gender roles, expectations, and societal norms. As women gained more agency in society, the portrayal of love in literature and media began to reflect evolving power dynamics and the pursuit of equality. Understanding these shifts can help us navigate the complexities of modern relationships and appreciate the progress made in achieving more balanced partnerships.

The Paradox of Idealized Love

In love's realm, enchanting tales we find,
Idealized portrayals, captivating minds.
But within the allure, a paradox we see,
Unrealistic expectations, a potential key.
For love, as painted in stories divine,
May lead to discontent, hearts left to pine.
The pedestal of perfection, a fragile illusion,
Unattainable standards, love's grand confusion.
Yet in this paradox, a wisdom gleams,
To balance idealism with grounded dreams.
For love's true beauty lies in its imperfections,
A dance of flaws and strengths, unique reflections.
Let us embrace the complexities that love brings,
The messy, imperfect, and all the heartstrings.
For in the reality of love's ebb and flow,
True fulfillment and growth begin to show.
Striving for a love rooted in authenticity,

Free from the shackles of idealized felicity.
Embracing the flaws, the quirks, and the strife,
Love blossoms in the tapestry of a real-life.
So let us find a balance, a middle ground,
Where love's ideals and reality are found.
In this delicate dance, we shall thrive,
With healthier, fulfilling love as our drive.

While love stories can be enchanting and inspiring, it is essential to acknowledge the potential drawbacks of idealized portrayals of love. Unrealistic expectations can lead to disappointment and dissatisfaction in relationships. It is important to strike a balance between the romantic ideals presented in love stories and the realities of everyday life. Embracing the imperfections and complexities of love can foster healthier and more fulfilling relationships.

Love and Self-Identity

Love stories, like mirrors, hold a key,
Reflecting desires, fears, and what may be.
Within their pages, we seek our own trace,
Embarking on journeys of self-embrace.
Through fictional characters, we find a kin,
Parallels to our lives, emotions within.
Their trials and triumphs, lessons untold,
Illuminate our path, our stories unfold.
In love's embrace, transformative might,
A catalyst for growth, shining bright.
Exploring our identities, we soar,
Love's tapestry revealing more.
Desires awaken, aspirations bloom,
Love's prism casting colors in every room.
We delve deeper, understanding deep,
Our emotions, desires, secrets we keep.
Through love's lens, self-discovery found,

Unraveling the mysteries, truths unbound.
Love stories guide, with wisdom to impart,
A journey within, a masterpiece of art.
So let us embrace these tales divine,
As mirrors reflecting our own design.
Love's transformative power we shall employ,
To understand ourselves and truly enjoy.

Love stories often serve as mirrors, reflecting our desires, aspirations, and fears. They can inspire individuals to explore their own identities and embark on journeys of self-discovery. Through the experiences of fictional characters, we may find parallels in our own lives, gaining insight into our emotions, desires, and personal growth. Love stories have the power to catalyze transformative experiences, helping us understand ourselves and our relationships better.

Love in Different Cultures

In cultures diverse, love's essence blooms,
Shaping its portrayal through unique rooms.
Perspectives on romance, so beautifully expressed,
In courtship's dance, each culture is blessed.
A tapestry woven with colors so rich,
Love's threads intertwine, a cultural niche.
From East to West, a world of love's embrace,
Embracing differences, celebrating each case.
For love knows no boundaries, it breaks the mold,
A universal language, as stories are told.
In every corner, love's essence prevails,
Through customs and traditions, it unveils.
In diverse expressions, love's beauty we find,
From grand gestures to subtleties refined.
It challenges the notion of a single decree,
A kaleidoscope of love, so wild and free.
So let us explore, with open hearts and minds,

Love's myriad expressions, the world binds.
For in cultural diversity, we truly see,
Love's boundless nature, in all its majesty.

Cultural diversity plays a significant role in shaping the portrayal of love. Different cultures have unique perspectives on romance, courtship, and relationship dynamics. Exploring love stories from various cultures allows us to appreciate the rich tapestry of human experiences and challenges the notion of a universal definition of love. It reminds us that love is a deeply personal and culturally influenced phenomenon, embracing a multitude of expressions and interpretations.

Love as a Universal Experience

Across the ages, love's ethereal dance,
A universal thread, we all have the chance.
Through different tongues and cultures vast,
Love's language echoes, from first to last.
In tender moments, hearts aligned,
Love's essence, eternal and unconfined.
It knows no borders, it knows no bounds,
In every soul, its presence resounds.
Emotions woven, hopes and dreams unfurled,
Love's tapestry, a testament to the world.
For in vulnerability, we find our strength,
Love's power unites, regardless of length.
From ancient tales to modern lore,
Love's story echoes forevermore.
A testament to our shared humanity,
Love's universal gift, an eternal serenity.
So let us celebrate, with hearts aglow,
Love's universal embrace, in highs and lows.
For in this journey, we all partake,
Love's universal language, our souls awake.

Despite the diversity in how love is perceived and expressed, it remains a universal experience that transcends time and cultural boundaries. Love stories, in their various forms, remind us of the shared human capacity to love and be loved. They capture the essence of our emotions, hopes, and vulnerabilities, reminding us of our common humanity. Love stories serve as a testament to the enduring power of this profound emotion throughout the ages.

The Power of Love Stories

In pages adorned with love's sweet prose,
Love stories bloom, their power grows.
They captivate and enchant, their magic profound,
Evoking emotions, emotions unbound.
From joy's embrace to tears' gentle flow,
Love stories take us on a journey, we bestow.
Through laughter and sorrow, they hold the key,
To the intricacies of human bonds, we see.
Across generations, their words endure,
Transcending time, their essence pure.
Love's tales whisper, timeless and grand,
Guiding hearts, as they reach out and expand.
With each turn of the page, a new chapter unfolds,
Love's power revealed, as the story unfolds.
For in love stories' embrace, we find solace and grace,
Shaping our perceptions, love's tender embrace.
So let us cherish these tales of love's might,
With open hearts, in their warm light.
For the power of love stories, steadfast and true,
Inspires our hearts, and transforms me and you.

Love stories possess a unique ability to captivate and inspire us. They evoke a wide range of emotions, from joy and laughter to sadness and introspection. Love stories help us explore the complexities of human relationships, offering insights into the human condition. Their timeless appeal lies in their ability to transcend time and space, resonating with audiences across generations. The power of love stories lies in their potential to touch our hearts and influence the way we perceive and experience love.

Love's Influence on Society

Love's influence on society, profound and wide,
Love stories shape the world, with every stride.
They challenge norms, redefine the known,
Expanding hearts, making prejudices disown.
Through diverse narratives, they light the way,
Portraying love's spectrum, in vibrant display.
Inclusive tales of love, breaking through walls,
Promoting empathy, as compassion calls.
With every page turned, a shift takes place,
Society awakened, embracing love's grace.
Gender roles reshaped, equality in sight,
Love stories pave the path, towards a brighter light.
Media and literature, the catalysts of change,
With stories that resonate, hearts rearrange.
Inclusive love stories, their power vast,
Creating a world where acceptance is cast.
So let love's influence shape society's quest,
With stories of love, we're truly blessed.
For in the realm of love, we can all find our role,
Building a world where love's acceptance is whole.

Love stories are not mere entertainment; they shape our societal norms, values, and aspirations. They have the power to challenge and redefine existing notions of love, relationships, and gender roles. By portraying diverse narratives and showcasing inclusive love stories, media and literature can contribute to positive social change. Love stories that promote empathy, understanding, and equality have the potential to foster a more inclusive and accepting society.

Conclusion

Love through the ages has been a subject of fascination and inspiration. Famous love stories, spanning from ancient times to modern literature and media, have left an indelible impact on our understanding of love and relationships. While they may not always reflect reality, these stories have the power to ignite our imagination, provoke thought, and touch our hearts. By critically analyzing the influence of love stories on modern relationships, we can navigate the complexities of love with a greater understanding and appreciation for the diverse narratives that shape our lives.

Don't miss out!

Visit the website below and you can sign up to receive emails whenever Rajesh Giri publishes a new book. There's no charge and no obligation.

https://books2read.com/r/B-A-OWRS-HKOJC

Connecting independent readers to independent writers.

Did you love *Love Through the Ages: The Impact of Famous Love Stories on Modern Relationships*? Then you should read *The Mind's Playground: Unlocking Your Potential through Academics*[1] by Rajesh Giri!

The Mind's Playground: Unlocking Your Potential through Academics is a comprehensive guide that provides practical strategies for academic success. This book covers a range of topics, including effective study techniques, time management, critical thinking and problem-solving, cross-cultural competence, and lifelong learning. It is an essential resource for students of all levels who want to maximize their academic potential and achieve their goals.

Some of the unique features of this book include:

---

1. https://books2read.com/u/4XwZjN

2. https://books2read.com/u/4XwZjN

- Comprehensive coverage of a range of topics essential for academic success
- Practical tips and strategies that can be easily implemented
- Interactive exercises and activities to enhance learning and understanding
- Real-world examples and case studies to illustrate key concepts
- Expert advice and insights from academics and industry professionals
- Easy-to-read format with clear and concise language

Why is this book a must-read?

- Provides a comprehensive guide for academic success that covers all essential topics
- Offers practical strategies and tips that can be easily implemented by students of all levels
- Provides expert advice and insights from academics and industry professionals to enhance learning and understanding
- Contains interactive exercises and activities that help readers engage with the material and apply it to their own lives
- Presents real-world examples and case studies that illustrate key concepts and demonstrate their practical application
- Is written in an easy-to-read format with clear and concise language that makes it accessible to a wide range of readers.

Also by Rajesh Giri

The Spiritual Journey To Jyotirlingas
The Spiritual Journey to Somnath Jyotirlinga

Standalone
Scamming in the Shoe Market: An Inside Look
Still In Love With Her: A Guide To Sustain in a Long-Term Relationship
Beyond Time and Space: A Love That Endures
Love at First Write: Balancing Love and Creativity
Broken Family Stronger Bond: The Power of a Divorced Daughter
Heartstrings: The Art of Loving Someone Who Can't Love You Back
The Phoenix Effect: Rebuilding Your Life After Adversity
Love's Illusion: When Falling Feels Like Flying
Back Bench Lovebirds: A Story of Young Love and Rebellions
Loving My Haters: Finding Strength in Adversity
The Silver Lining of Heartbreak: A Journey to Love
The Mind's Playground: Unlocking Your Potential through Academics
Creating Boundaries with Art: A Guide to Remove Toxic Friends from Your Life
Beyond the Hate: Embracing Love and Forgiveness
Love Through the Ages: The Impact of Famous Love Stories on Modern Relationships

About the Author

Rajesh Kumar Giri is a renowned lecturer of Mathematics, content writer, and a Practical Success Coach. With a passion for writing academic and educational content, Rajesh guides and trains people worldwide, breaking the barriers of language and region with his simple and easy-to-understand writing skills.

Rajesh's journey began in a poor family in a remote area of West Champaran, where he faced numerous challenges in paying for higher education. Despite the obstacles, he persevered and completed his degree, taking his first steps towards educating people and sharing his rags-to-riches ideas. Today, he resides in New Delhi, the capital of India, with his beautiful wife and two lovely sons, and he remains dedicated to serving poor students by providing free education online and offline.

Rajesh has been writing content in the education, affiliate marketing, and health niches since 2006. He believes that experiences speak louder than imaginary and bookish ideas, and his words connect with readers and result in conversions. As a Practical Success Coach, he helps people overcome their limiting beliefs and achieve their goals through practical techniques and strategies.

With his wealth of experience and passion for writing, Rajesh is committed to helping people around the world unlock their full potential and achieve success in all areas of their lives.